SACRED DESIRE

SACRED DESIRE

Growing in Compassionate Living

Nancy K. Morrison, MD
Sally K. Severino, MD

Templeton Foundation Press
West Conshohocken, Pennsylvania

Templeton Foundation Press
300 Conshohocken State Road, Suite 670
West Conshohocken, PA 19428
www.templetonpress.org

Book design and composition by Scribe Typography

LIBRARY OF CONGRESS CATALOGING-IN-PUBLICATION DATA

Morrison, Nancy K.
Sacred desire: growing in compassionate living / Nancy K. Morrison and Sally K. Severino.
    p. cm.
Includes index.
ISBN-13: 978-1-59947-150-1 (alk. paper)
ISBN-10: 1-59947-150-7 (alk. paper)
1. Love—Religious aspects.   2. Desire—Religious aspects.
3. Compassion—Religious aspects.   I. Severino, Sally K.   II. Title.
BL626.4.M67 2009
205′.677—dc22

                                                    2008031614

Printed in the United States of America

09 10 11 12 13 14 10 9 8 7 6 5 4 3 2 1

To all the Sisters of Charity
for whom the love of Jesus urges them
to bring their redemptive attuning into the world
most especially,
Sister Linda Chavez, SC
Sister Mary Aloys Powell, SCL
Sister Rose Therese Wich, SC

   —Nancy K. Morrison

To my sons
Andrew Lawrence Severino
Michael John Severino
and grandsons
Travis Connelly Severino
Sundance Connelly Severino
Kai Connelly Severino
Joseph Lawrence Severino
whose love heals

   —Sally K. Severino

The century that is ending has been preoccupied with nucleic acids and proteins. The next one will concentrate on memory and desire. Will it be able to answer the questions they pose?

—François Jacob, *Of Flies, Mice and Men*

Contents

Foreword

SEVERAL YEARS AGO, I received a letter from someone I'd never met, asking me to consider co-writing a book. Though I was busy with my own manuscript—too busy, I suspected, to even consider working on a joint project with people I didn't know—I was intrigued enough by the proposal outlined in the letter that I agreed to fly to New Mexico to meet the authors in person. Thus began an amazing three-day conversation with two longtime psychiatrists whose private and professional lives were "not one," as Sally would put it, but also "not two." Early on in our talks, I realized that their serious commitment to science and the practice of medicine was absolutely interfused by their equally deep commitment to the practice of silent prayer. And this fascinated me.

Our discussion began around Nancy's dining-room table in a book-lined, rambling Victorian near downtown Albuquerque, filled to capacity with healthy plants, happy dogs, and countless musical scores. We picked it up again in Sally's Taos-style home overlooking the great high desert valley, a space whose elegant simplicity reminded me of the guest house at Christ in the Desert Monastery. Here indeed were two interesting human beings, seemingly not much alike, who had nevertheless found their intellectual and creative endeavors much enhanced by collaboration.

As they described their work to me, painstakingly unpacking for this woefully uninformed lit major the neurological back-stories of emotional states like fear and love, I found myself thinking of Psalm 139: "For you created my inmost being; you knit me together in my mother's womb. I praise you because I am fearfully and wonderfully made" (13–14). What they had come to realize through years of clinical work and professional study, they told me, is that we humans truly *are* designed for loving and being loved. Even more amazingly, we are *neurologically* designed for communion with God. This was delightful news, particularly in an era that more often than not uses science to denigrate, rather than validate, the claims of religion.

As fascinating as I found their work, however, several things quickly became clear: first, these two were already so "resonantly attuned" as creative partners that a lay third party would simply be an intrusion and an impediment, and, second, they were far more spiritually adventurous than I. Their mentors included controversial pioneers like Matthew Fox and John Shelby Spong; mine were C. S. Lewis and Pope Benedict the XVI. They visualized a world in which all religions, including Christianity, were ultimately revealed as one; I was and still am utterly convinced of the uniqueness and superiority of orthodox Christianity over all other religions.

Yet two years after that marvelous brainstorming session in the desert, I am thankful indeed that they went ahead with this project on their own. For they have marvelous riches to share—riches that nonscientists would be hard-pressed to uncover without their gracious help, riches that I am convinced have very much to do with "the mystery hidden for long ages past" (Rom. 16:25). More, what they have to teach can enlighten and instruct *everyone*—regardless of his or her religious or metaphysical beliefs—who longs to be a better, more compassionate human being. In this sense, Sally Severino and Nancy Morrison are like spiritual midwives, coaxing us forth into the light of our better selves. And for this good work of theirs, I personally owe them a great debt of gratitude.

Paula Huston

Introduction

> He [God/the Divine] alone is our desire and our life,
> and nothing else can give us any joy.
>
> —THOMAS MERTON

O UR TRAINING AS PSYCHIATRISTS has given us a valuable insight into the contemplative side of our being. Although we walked different paths, both led us to the same point of view. Both of us see sacred Desire as the force that urges us to fullness of life.

During most of my adult life, I (Sally) lived as two separate selves: my professional self as a psychiatrist and my private self as a person of faith. While each had its own integrity, I could never bring them together into oneness of being. Then in my late fifties, two events changed me forever.

On the professional level, mirror neurons were discovered. Mirror neurons are special cells that activate in our brains when we see another person do or feel something, just as they activate when we do or feel the same. This means that we are biologically equipped to relate on a very basic level by resonating with others' actions and emotions. This scientific discovery gave me one way to understand how we are able to read each other's minds and how we can grasp the intentions of others through direct simulation— by feeling, not by thinking. Because direct simulation occurs automatically and is not conscious, it gave me something physically embedded in me but beyond my will—something I could rely on—to account for interrelatedness. Here was my biological link to others and to God.

Simultaneous with this discovery in my professional life, a friend handed me Thomas Keating's book *Open Mind, Open Heart.* Keating introduced me to contemplative prayer, "a process of interior transformation, a conversation initiated by God and leading, if we consent, to divine union."[1] Contemplative prayer is a Christian method of mindfulness practice that is similar to methods practiced by other traditions such as Buddhist meditation, Taoist tai-chi, and Hindu yoga.[2] During the daily practice of contemplative prayer, my way of seeing reality changed.[3] This confirmed for me that not only did my mirror neurons allow me to respond to others by feeling them, my mirror neurons also allowed me to respond to the Divine Presence in and beyond all that exists.

My professional and faith selves integrated.

My (Nancy's) path, though different from Sally's, brought me to a similar place of professional and faith integration. The Roman Catholic Church wouldn't allow me to become a priest, and being a nun wasn't for me. I wasn't suited to scrubbing the bishop's house, especially when he was giving a party to which the nuns weren't invited. Instead, I turned to nature, which I loved, and became a scientist. The science that most excited me was the study of the mind, and so I specialized in psychiatry.

While my professional experience taught me about the ravages of terror in patients who suffered abuse, my personal living with breast cancer taught me about the distorting power of anxiety. Scientific studies confirmed what I felt and observed. They showed that people in a state of anxiety use their limbic/midbrain to process information. In doing so, people cannot think flexibly, and their thinking becomes superstitious, colored by frightful imaginings. People in a state of terror use their brain-stem/autonomic nervous system to process information in ways that are reactionary, knee-jerk responses. These states, over time, become the traits that characterize us.

I wanted to help my patients overcome the wounds of abuse, and I wanted to prevent my own anxiety from becoming a permanent trait. As sometimes happens, a crisis provokes an inspiration. My cancer motivated me to pick up the telephone and call Sister Mary Aloys, the Catholic nun who had been my spiritual mentor since I was a teenager. She suggested that I try contemplative prayer. It turned my life around.

I have continued this prayer practice with Sister Linda and Sister Rose Therese. It has taught me that in the spiritual realm something could be "real," such as my encounter with the Divine, and not be scientifically "measurable." It was, however, behaviorally verifiable in the way I lived with and beyond cancer. No longer did I react solely from anxiety. I could also live calmly and respond to life's throes with trust. I could help my patients do likewise.

The integration of our professional and faith selves opened both of us to sacred Desire. But what exactly is "Sacred Desire?"

The word "desire" most simply means: "to long or hope for." We may long for a relationship or a fast new car. We may hope for peace in the world or a new, more satisfying job. But the Latin root of desire, *desiderare*, reveals a deeper meaning: *de* is translated as "from" [or down, away] and *sider, sidus* as "heavenly body." Desire, then, literally "comes from the stars," which in ancient times signified the celestial powers, or the Divine. We are referring to this deeper meaning in this book. To denote that, we spell Desire with a capital "D." Our Desire in its purest form reflects our longing to be one with the Divine—the life force that creates and animates all that is.

Our understanding of "sacred" comes from the twentieth-century iconoclast Ivan Illich, who links "*sacrum*, the Latin noun . . . to . . . *sacred*," such that sacred is "the doorway to the absolute other, the place of self-revelation of the holy."[4] A synonym for *sacred* is *holy*. We use *sacred*, therefore, to mean the threshold at which our Desire meets the ultimate Holy (Yahweh in Jewish terms, God in Christian terms, Allah in Muslim terms, *Atman* in Hindu terms, Buddha nature in Buddhist terms).

Desire draws us to the threshold of the ultimate Holy, where we can respond to the spiritual and manifest it in compassion. This is sacred Desire, which we experience incarnated in us and mediated by our mirror neurons.

Sacred Desire: Growing in Compassionate Living springs from our shared conviction that Desire is the powerful urge that brings us into relationships that form our lives. This conviction shapes the chapters that follow. In chapter 1, we look at the biophysical and spiritual foundations of sacred Desire. In chapter 2, we see that newborn infants are born biologically equipped with the capacity to express their Desire and to interact with the Desire of their caregivers. When the newborn's Desire is met with love, joy results and fuels Desire for more compassionate relational experiences.

Newborn infants are also biologically equipped for self-preservation and fight/flight or freeze behavior. When Desire is met with fear, the biology that fear triggers leads us into out-of-control behaviors such as addiction, lust, and gluttony. We focus on the growth of Desire developmentally (chapter 3) and socially (chapter 4), before exploring how Desire can be distorted (chapter 5) and reconfigured (chapters 6 and 7). We continue Desire's journey into redemptive action within us—expressed psychologically as bringing us from distortedness to wholeness, biologically as bringing us from fight/flight or freeze to calm and connection, spiritually as bringing us from brokenness to holiness (chapter 8)—and within community, expressed as bringing us from self-protective to species-protective behavior (chapter 9). We close in chapter 10 by exploring the implications of sacred Desire for the peaceful preservation and nurturance of our world community and our planet.

We invite you to embrace sacred Desire and to be willing to be surprised at what can result when we ask ourselves, "How do we live most fully from our sacred Desire for the Divine?"

SACRED DESIRE

CHAPTER 1

WOMB OF COMPASSION

The Beginning of Life and Love

> From all eternity God [the Divine] lies on a maternity bed giving birth. The essence of God [the Divine] is birthing.
>
> — MEISTER ECKHART

THAT OUR LIFE BEGINS IN LOVE is beautifully conveyed in Hebrew, where the word for compassion or mercy, *rachamim*, comes from the same root as the word meaning womb, *rechem*.[1] The view of the Divine as "womb of compassion" captures the vast benevolence that underlies all of creation, including our own coming into being. It also exemplifies how all of life is relational—from the relationship between the Divine and nature, between the Divine and humans, between parent and child, and between body and mind and spirit as told herein.

As Jeannie B., speaking of her first pregnancy, put it, "I felt like the three of us—my husband, my baby, and I—were all caught up in the wonder of the Divine." Like Jeannie, we are sometimes acutely aware (just as we are also sometimes utterly unaware) of this wonder, this manifestation of our relationship with the Divine that is expressed as love.

Often parents manifest this love in particularly strong and compelling ways, even before a child is born. Shortly after Peg S.

learned she was pregnant, someone asked her if she planned to keep the baby. "Of course, I'm going to keep the baby!" she cried, her response immediate and visceral like a power potion coursing through her body.[2] Looking back, Peg comments, "It was almost as if my own life was threatened." Her body spontaneously readied her to protect the inviolable connectedness that she felt within her for her baby.

Peg's love of and connection with the life growing inside her vitally illustrates the womb of compassion—what Jewish scholar Avivah Gottlieb Zornberg calls "the space of desire, the hollow of holiness."[3] In a very unexpected way, Peg's love of the life in her space of desire led her to a deeper love of herself. "I felt precious to have this child within me," she says. "It was an honor to carry this child."

The womb itself is inherently compassionate. While we live in the womb, we are kept warm without clothing and nourished without eating. We don't even need to breathe. All of our needs in utero are met without our effort.[4]

In addition to a baby growing, much happens during pregnancy. Biologically, Mother's hormones are changing. Psychologically, Mother is imagining her baby and forming a mother mind-set. Spiritually, Mother is developing a spirit-set about being a mother and about her relationship with her baby. Socially, Father and extended family are offering the support that allows this psychobiospiritual experience to blossom.

One mother—quoted by infant researcher Daniel Stern and his psychiatrist wife, Nadia Bruschweiler-Stern—gives us a glimpse of the mind-set and spirit-set she is developing. During her fourth month of gestation when she felt her baby kick, she said, "It's as if this baby kicks in accordance with my moods, like he's already tuned in to me." According to the Sterns, "The imagined baby is, of course, purely subjective, so the same kick could inspire the mother to imagine any . . . possible character traits."[5]

Peg, whom we met earlier, did not talk about her imaginary baby, but she did say, "I still felt precious even after he was out of my body. I'd never thought of it that way before, and that sense of preciousness remained." In Peg's sense of preciousness, she experienced the womb as compassionate in a very palpable way that nourished her spirit-set for motherhood.

Giving birth—like pregnancy—was a spiritual experience for Peg, but she was totally unprepared for the immensity of that experience. "Everyone wanted to prepare me for the pain, the panic," she remembered. But Peg's experience of giving birth included more than her labor pains. "*Nobody* told me how giving

THE HOLY NECTAR

When experiencing safety, our body produces a biochemical named oxytocin—what we are calling a holy nectar—that appears in our bloodstream as a hormone and in our brain as a signaling substance (called neurotransmitter). This nectar

- Makes us calm and friendly
- Activates our parasympathetic nervous system that decreases our blood pressure and increases our digestion
- Gives us trust and security to bond positively with others

Unlike most hormones that shut off their own production, oxytocin does the opposite. The presence of oxytocin triggers the production of more oxytocin. In other words, we are made so that we can't run out of love. The more we have, the more we get. The more we get, the more we live in the physiology underlying our trust of Desire.

Source: Kerstin Uvnas Moberg, *The Oxytocin Factor: Tapping the Hormone of Calm, Love, and Healing* (Cambridge, Mass.: Da Capo Press, 2003), x–xii, 4.

birth would be an experience of ecstasy," she continued. "I was afraid people would think I was crazy if I told them." Indeed, science now confirms what Peg felt. She literally was infused with the Holy. A holy nectar, a term we coined, pervaded her being, promoting her feeling of ecstasy and also producing her uterine contractions.[6]

Mothers, nonmothers, fathers, and nonfathers know "womb" experiences—hollow of holiness experiences, space of desire experiences. Womb experiences demand that we take seriously the fact that our bodies are made to be spirit-nurturers for one another. Linda L., remembering when she was pregnant with her now-teenaged son, says, "What surprised me about pregnancy was what a huge responsibility it was to be carrying life inside me. I realized that anything I did to my body affected my child." She worried about all the things she should or shouldn't do, including what she should eat or not eat. Then someone told her that whatever she ate, the nutrients the baby needed would go to the baby first, then to her. "It was such a great joy to have a baby," Linda continued, "but also a great relief to know that my body would give the baby what he needed." As Linda experienced relief when learning that the whole responsibility for the well-being of her child was not hers alone, she experienced the reality of being a spirit-nurturer.

As infants, once held and fed by our mother's womb, we enter the world with full potential to become spirit-nurturers (as well as the potential to be sidetracked from this destiny). How our potentials develop depends, normally, on how we are welcomed by our mothers and other caregivers. In this sense, the womb of compassion is our human capacity to be spirit-nurturers for one another. We are not whole alone. Our being and becoming—physical, psychological, and spiritual—are fed (or starved) in relationship with those around us.

We literally *are* relationship. As cell biologist Bruce Lipton puts it, "You may consider yourself an individual, but . . . I can tell you

THE POWER POTION

When confronted by a threat (real or imagined), our body produces a power potion composed of hormones and neurotransmitters—such as adrenaline, noradrenalin, and vasopressin—that prepares us to either fight or flee. This is the physiology of self-protective behaviors. Our power potion

- Makes us angry, afraid, or both
- Activates our sympathetic nervous system that increases our blood pressure and decreases our digestion
- Gives us power to focus on defending against threat

When chronically aroused, this cocktail is the physiology underlying our mistrust of Desire.

Source: Kerstin Uvnas Moberg, *The Oxytocin Factor: Tapping the Hormone of Calm, Love, and Healing* (Cambridge, Mass.: Da Capo Press, 2003), ix–x, 5.

that you are in truth a cooperative community of approximately 50 trillion single-celled citizens. . . . As a nation reflects the traits of its citizens, our human-ness must reflect the basic nature of our cellular communities."[7]

Phyllis Tickle articulates the relationship of our physical, psychological, and spiritual aspects in a slightly different way. In reflecting on one of her pregnancies, Tickle writes:

> I don't know who in the late twentieth century decided to take the traditional trichotomy of body versus mind versus spirit and popularize it into the unified buzz phrase of "Body, Mind, and Spirit," but I do know it was definitely a woman and definitely a woman who had been pregnant. . . . The degree of fusion among body, mind, and spirit early in midpregnancy is not an emotion; it is a translation . . . into an ecstatic way of being that is more like existing within the aura

of a great radiance. . . . The prayers of early to midpregnancy rise . . .
to some Completeness, to some Magnificence.[8]

Sacred Desire urges us toward wholeness, or, in Tickle's words,
toward "some Completeness . . . some Magnificence."[9] It urges us
to fulfill what we are designed to be—persons who live and love
graciously, freely, and fully in relationship.

Yet, paradoxically, we do not begin—or carry out—our journey
as "unwhole" people. Throughout our life journey we are whole,
though we don't always know it or act like it. The Divine lives in
our DNA, alludes Francis S. Collins, leading geneticist and head
of the Human Genome Project, when he quotes C. S. Lewis, "If

OXYTOCIN AND VASOPRESSIN: THE BIOCHEMISTRY OF ATTACHMENT

Both oxytocin and vasopressin are essential for human well-being.
What is important is keeping in balance the two physiological conditions that they produce: calm and connection in balance with
fight or flight.

- Oxytocin and vasopressin are closely related in chemical composition and are found in all mammals.
- Oxytocin and vasopressin are produced in the hypothalamus of
  the brain.
- The female sex hormone estrogen reinforces the influence of
  oxytocin and produces longer-lasting effects in females.
- In rats it takes twice the amount of oxytocin in males and in
  females without ovaries to produce the same effect as that
  found in females with normal estrogen levels.

Source: Kerstin Uvnas Moberg, *The Oxytocin Factor: Tapping the Hormone of
Calm, Love, and Healing* (Cambridge, Mass.: Da Capo Press, 2003), 61, 74.

there was a controlling power outside the universe . . . [t]he only way in which we could expect it to show itself would be inside ourselves as an influence or a command trying to get us to behave in a certain way."[10]

The challenge and the opportunity of our lives is to live from that command—that is, to reveal and express the Divine within us.[11] In short, from the beginning of life and with our mothers, we are co-creating ourselves in a womb of compassion to live out of and into our deepest Desire. We are co-creating ourselves both in our being (our Desire for the Holy) and in our doing (our Desire to express the Holy within us and among us). The practical implications for this are far-reaching. If we truly love in our being and in our actions, the world will be transformed even as we are transformed.

But the journey toward becoming and living out of our true essence is not always an easy one. Life experiences, cultural and familial influences, distortedness and pain dim our spiritual vision so that it is difficult to recognize the presence of the Divine around us and even more difficult to recognize the spiritual *within* us. Instead of experiencing wholeness of being that cannot be moved from its sacred center of enduring love, we feel fragmented by life's throes and our own interior struggles. Instead of living in a world of compassion, we live in a world of violence. Instead of growing in love and freely manifesting our sacred Desire, we grow in fear and manifest our ego.

How, then, do we reorient our lives toward our deepest Desire— to express the Divine within us, to become who we are meant to be, and to become one with the sacred, which is love?

One avenue, through which life holds us close in the womb of compassion, is in the love and caring of others. In the next chapter we will explore how the seeds of Desire grow when we are infants and discover that, no matter how difficult our lives may have been, there is hope for a fuller and freer life.

CHAPTER 2

THE GRACE OF GAZING

> The power of new life is in the gaze. The face of the
> mother is the harbinger of life for the child, and the
> face of the child is a refreshing and renewing spring
> for those willing to look.
>
> —DANIEL O'CONNOR, "GAZING AT THE
> MOTHER'S FACE"

IDEALLY, WE BEGIN LIFE in the "Yes" of two people's eyes. With the birth of a child, the lovers who once gazed only at each other now widen the grace of their gazing. In awe at the miracle before them, the mother or father holds the child close and gazes into the little one's eyes—and the child gazes back. In this moment, two become one.

This loving gaze seems natural—and it is.[1] But much more happens in this gaze than, dare we say, meets the eye. Though infants were once considered unfortunate because they enter life helpless and nearsighted, we now know that an infant's vision is perfect for seeing its mother's face while snuggled in her arms.[2] And here—in this seemingly simple act of love, of mother and child gazing at each other—the brain is literally being "wired" as new neural pathways and connections are created. These positive emotional exchanges between mother and infant shape the brain, not just of the infant but also of the mother (or other loving caregiver).[3]

But what goes on in the gaze is not simply the creation of neural pathways. A pathway to fullness of life is also being created.

Gazing at each other mediates the flow of creative energy as mother and infant experience and share ongoing love. Without knowing it, the mother says "Yes" to life through her gaze—and her infant gazes that "Yes" back to her. For the mother, this "Yes" offers a fresh opportunity to re-experience (or perhaps experience in a new way) profound love, hope, and trust. This intimate encounter often leads to a deepened or even new concern for the world as a whole. These cherished moments may reaffirm and strengthen her faith, or—in the case of someone without previous spiritual grounding or one whose faith experiences have been negative and deeply hurtful—may initiate an unexpected spiritual longing or awareness.

In turn, as the mother conveys this life-affirming "Yes" to her child, she creates the infant's first experience of being valued. For the infant, these early "Yes" moments lay the foundation for valuing in all relationships. This is the beginning of what James Fowler calls a "covenantal pattern of relationship," for we always live our lives in relationship with others.[4] Here, too, the seeds of Desire begin to germinate.

What happens in the gaze (or tender touching, rocking, singing, talking, smiling) continues what happened in the womb of compassion: the creation of life and love. We call this creative exchange "resonant attuning." In a general sense, to attune means to bring into harmony or to make aware or responsive. Resonant attuning is similar to "being present" to another, but it goes far beyond that. It brings two beings into dynamic harmony with each other. Instantaneously and unconsciously, they exchange vital information (sensations, states of mind, their very *being*) and energy (physical, emotional, spiritual).

When the two beings are a mother and infant, the exchange of resonant attuning lays the foundation for the development of the infant's capacity for understanding his or her physical, emotional, and spiritual self as well as the capacity for empathy with others. In this caring experience of calm and peacefulness—what

ATTUNING

Our concept of attuning builds on what we have known since the 1970s as the way we share internal feeling states with each other. Infant researcher Daniel Stern and his colleagues call it *affect attunement*. They indicate that affect attunement involves some form of matching—in this instance between mother and infant—where mother's external behavior expresses the match of her internal emotional state with the internal emotional state of her infant. The process occurs rapidly, largely out of awareness and almost automatically.

We prefer the verb *attuning* because it emphasizes that the process is an active one whereby parents nonverbally know and reflect back to their infant the infant's own experience. It is a special form of social perception and communication.

Our concept of attuning builds on what we know about the limbic brain, which specializes in detecting and analyzing the internal state of others. *Limbic resonance* is the term used by psychiatrists Lewis, Amini, and Lannon, who build their general theory of love upon this concept.

By using the term *resonant attuning,* which takes the process beyond the limbic system, we emphasize the connection of the limbic system down to the brainstem vagal system and up to the frontal cortex. We postulate that mirror neurons in the cortex mediate attuning. We also extend our concept of attuning beyond the mind and brain realms to the realm of the spiritual. Here we postulate that the same mind and body functions that allow us to connect with each other also allow us to connect with nature and the creative life force.

Sources: Daniel N. Stern, Lynne Hofer, Wendy Haft, and John Dore, "Affect Attunement: The Sharing of Feeling States between Mother and Infant by means of Inter-modal Fluency," *Social Perception in Infants,* ed. Tiffany M. Field and Nathan A. Fox (Norwood, N.J.: Ablex Publishing, 1985), 249–68; Thomas Lewis, Fari Amini, and Richard Lannon, *A General Theory of Love* (New York: Random House, 2000).

we might call "holy harmony"—the infant is "learning *through*" Mother and is "responding to the-world-according-to" Mother. (At this point, because the infant lacks language, learning is body learning.) "They [infants] 'know' the other person . . . in the sense that they can look at the other and relate to her attitudes, or they can observe her behaviour and register enough about her actions to copy them."[5] We believe that, in part, they are able to do this—to attune resonantly to others—because they have mirror neurons in their brains. Mirror neurons allow infants automatically to be moved by others' behaviors, emotions, and attitudes.

When an infant is in distress—hungry, thirsty, or soiled—and the mother appropriately relieves this distress, neural pathways are developed in the infant's brain that affirm and substantiate that a movement from distress to comfort is possible. In other words, through relieving the infant's distress in some concrete way, the mother lays a foundation for experiences of hope, trust, and love. These neural pathways become essential when, later in life, we experience physical, psychological, or spiritual distress. Our experience as infants enables us to sense that something—or someone—exists beyond our immediate distress. That knowledge both sustains us and gives us hope in the midst of our distress. Dag Hammarskjöld summed up the spiritual implications of this sacred experience when he wrote, "I don't know Who—or what—put the question, I don't even know when it was put. I don't even remember answering. But at some moment I did answer *Yes* to Someone—or Something—and from that hour I was certain that existence is meaningful and that, therefore, my life, in self-surrender, had a goal."[6]

Resonant attuning is a powerful spiritual experience for both the mother and the infant because they are never alone in their attuning. Here, the Divine is palpably manifested in the experience of resonant attuning in relationship. This mutual, interactive exchange of feelings, energy, and being enables us to grow in compassion. This is the grace of gazing.

A friend of ours tells this story about the grace of gazing:

> A few years ago, my good friends Cathy and Ben were expecting their
> first child and chose not to have the baby's gender revealed to them
> before the birth. When their little girl was born, Ben—very briefly
> —was disappointed. An avid outdoorsman, he had wanted a son to
> share his love of nature and outdoor activities and, I suspect, to have a
> relationship with his son unlike the difficult one he had with his own
> father. A day or two after their daughter's birth, I called Cathy and
> Ben's home and got their answering machine. Ben's voice, ordinar-
> ily laconic and laid back, was animated and bright as he announced
> the birth of little Alexandra—and, oh yes, he added, leave a message if
> you want to. A day or two later when my husband and I visited Cathy,

GAZING: MEDIATED BY BRAIN MIRROR NEURONS

In the last decade of the twentieth century, scientists discovered
mirror neurons in the brains of monkeys. Because scientific studies of recording from single brain neurons in humans is a rare procedure, the existence of mirror neurons in humans has not yet
been confirmed directly. Indirectly, abundant evidence supports a
mirror-neuron system in humans. Data comes from neurophysiological and brain-imaging experiments. We believe that mirror neurons may be the key to what happens during gazing.

As we watch the behaviors or emotions of another, our mirror
neurons light up as if we were performing that action or feeling
that emotion. Our activated mirror neurons give us an embodied
simulation of the other person. What we see another do, we have
done. What we see another feel, we have felt.

During gazing, mirror neurons likely support emotional resonance and spiritual attuning by

- Mediating communication between others and us

Ben, and Alexandra, Ben's brief disappointment was long gone. Like Cathy, he held their little girl tenderly and gazed into her eyes. Little Alexandra, I thought, had quickly—and completely—won over both Ben and Cathy. Clearly the spiritual was present here and was being manifested powerfully and exquisitely in the grace of their gazing and their new, yet already great, love for one another.

We are truly created to do amazing things with our brains, being, and bodies. Like little Alexandra, at the moment we're born, we're ready to attune with other human beings. Over fifty years ago, psychiatrist Harry Stack Sullivan spoke of the necessity of "tender cooperation" in caring for a child.[7] The mother's tender cooperation is her adapting to her infant's moment-to-

- Changing each other's internal biological state
- Influencing the long-term construction of each other's brains

While other animals—monkeys, dolphins, dogs, probably apes, and possibly elephants—have mirror neurons, human beings with our large brains and growing complexity have a greater capacity to form concepts about inherently unobservable things. The ultimate unobservable is, of course, God or the Divine.

Sources: Sarah-Jayne Blakemore and Jean Decety, "From the Perception of Action to the Understanding of Intention," *Nature Reviews Neuroscience* 2 (2001): 561–67; Louis Cozolino, *The Neuroscience of Human Relationships: Attachment and the Developing Social Brain* (New York: W. W. Norton, 2006); Vittorio Gallese, L. Fadiga, L. Fogassi, and Giacomo Rizzolatti, "Action Recognition in the Premotor Cortex," *Brain* 119 (1996): 593–609; Vittorio Gallese, M. N. Eagle, and P. Migone, "Intentional Attunement: Mirror Neurons and the Neural Underpinnings of Interpersonal Relations," *Journal of the American Psychoanalytic Association* 55, no. 1 (2007): 131–76; Daniel John Povinelli, "Behind the Ape's Appearance: Escaping Anthropocentrism in the Study of Other Minds," *Daedalus* 133, no. 1 (2004): 29–41; Giacomo Rizzolatti and Laila Craighero, "The Mirror-Neuron System," *Annual Review Neuroscience* 27 (2004): 169–92.

IMAGINE YOUR BRAIN

You can imagine your brain by taking your right hand and making a fist with your thumb placed inside your other fingers. As you look at your fist with your thumb facing you, you are seeing an image of what your right brain would look like if you cut your brain from top to bottom through the middle and then looked at the right half from its inside.

Your four fingers represent the cortex of your brain. Our human cortex (the thinking and organizing part of our brain) is more highly developed than that of any other mammal. Your thumb, covered by your fingers, represents the limbic system (our emotional brain). The area from your thumb to your wrist represents the brain stem (our instinctual brain), which is the source of the autonomic nervous system. The area from your wrist to your elbow represents the spinal cord. Taken together, our cortex, limbic brain, brain stem, and spinal cord are called the central nervous system.

Source: Daniel J. Siegel, *The Developing Mind: Toward a Neurobiology of Interpersonal Experience* (New York: Guilford, 1999), 11–12.

moment changing needs. Through this tender cooperation, both the baby's brain and the foundation of the baby's spiritual life begin to develop. Very literally, in holding her child a mother holds the inner life—psychological, biophysical, and spiritual—of her child and influences its unfolding. As she gazes and comforts her infant by rocking, a mother engages the potential of her infant's brain and helps it to develop. In particular, her interaction with her infant nurtures first the development of the autonomic nervous system (which governs involuntary actions such as breathing and heartbeat), then the limbic system including amygdala and hippocampus (the brain's emotional and memory centers), and finally the prefrontal cortex (the "organizing" part of the brain).

To greatly simplify a complex biophysical and neurological process, the ventral vagal system is at work here. The vagal nerve, known as the "wandering nerve" because it "wanders" all over our bodies, plays a role in digesting our food, slowing our heart rate, *and* in our capacity to attune to and with others. Occurring only in mammals, the ventral vagal system makes social engagement and bonding possible.[8] Gazing, rocking, singing, touching, and smiling activate this system, so as a mother tends her child, the bond—biophysical and neurological as well as spiritual—grows. Eventually this leads to an experience of joy.

For the infant, of course, this experience of joy is wordless. This may at least partially explain why, when we feel joyful, the feeling is so visceral that we often have difficulty explaining it. Most likely our joy has triggered a "felt," or preverbal, memory of joy we experienced early in life—probably during our first year of life.[9] Joy becomes part of the infant's body wisdom or knowledge, what we might call a "visceral knowing." The baby experiences this physically—without awareness of separateness or conflict (thus, an experience of "oneness")—and with a strong sense of security. Although the infant lacks the capacity to articulate the experience in words, it carries that experience deep within, creating the neural capacity and body knowledge for later entering into and recognizing other experiences of oneness. Experiences of oneness are emphatically not absorption, not a loss of being. It is more like the oneing of two people in marriage.[10]

The experience of resonant attuning in infancy—and the sense of security and safety that accompanies it—remains with us as we grow older. Ultimately it remains with us throughout our lives. The love shared in gazing has surprising power, as we see in Sally's experience many years ago with her then nine-month-old son Mike:

> I'll never forget that early summer evening. My adorable Mike, who had experienced nine months of two parents and four grandparents

THE NERVOUS SYSTEM

The nervous system is divided into the central and the peripheral nervous systems.

1. Central Nervous System
   - Brain

     Cortex: organizes experiences

     Limbic System: emotions, memory (autobiographical narrative), attachment

     Brain stem: reflexes

   - Spinal Cord: brain-body communication

2. Peripheral Nervous System
   - Autonomic Nervous System: automatically maintains body functions

     Sympathetic: speeds up body functions and responds to perceived danger

     Parasympathetic: slows down body functions
     Dorsal Vagus: responds to life threat
     Ventral Vagus: responds to social cues
     (Ventral Vagus is unique to mammals.)

   - Somatic Nervous System: muscle movement

Sources: Louis Cozolino, *The Neuroscience of Human Relationships: Attachment and the Developing Social Brain* (New York: W. W. Norton, 2006); Stephen W. Porges, "Love: An Emergent Property of the Mammalian Autonomic Nervous System," *Psychoneuroendocrinology* 23 (1998): 837–61; Stephen W. Porges, "The Polyvagal Theory: Phylogenetic Substrates of a Social Nervous System," *International Journal of Psychophysiology* 42 (2001): 123–46.

doting on him, slipped while we were playing outdoors. Instinctively I grabbed him by the leg to keep him from hitting his head on the concrete patio. I saved him from hitting his head but unfortunately broke his leg in the process. Mike cried uncontrollably as my husband and I frantically tried to reach Dr. Engel, Mike's pediatrician. By the time we got to the emergency room, Mike was asleep in my arms comforted by my closeness.

"That child can't possibly have a broken bone," exclaimed Dr. Engel, when he saw us in the examining room.

"You'll see," I replied. "Just wait until you move him." Dr. Engel quickly discovered that Mike's femur was, indeed, fractured.

Although I felt overwhelmingly sorry for having "caused" Mike's broken leg, I could also see—as I held him and watched him, relaxed and sleeping—the power of our loving bond. Somehow the comfort of being held in my arms overcame the pain in his little body.

Looking back I am astounded, as was Mike's pediatrician, that a child with a broken leg could fall asleep. Now I realize that this was a clear result of our shared experiences of resonant attuning. Neurologically, his experience of me as a source of his well-being had prepared his brain to override his acute pain while he was in my arms.

Obviously, resonant attuning with our children will not protect them from all experiences of pain—physical, emotional, or spiritual. But it will strengthen the capacity, as it did for little Mike, to be all right *despite* the pain.

As you've been reading, you may have been wondering about all the children—perhaps including yourself—who did not receive such a loving welcome into the world. Sometimes these ideas stir concerns about our own parenting and how we attuned to our own children. While most of us were good enough mothers or fathers, we sometimes worry about the times we fell short.

Children who receive no loving care, no cherishing gaze, literally may not survive.[11] The good news is, a child who survives infancy and toddlerhood has received enough (though perhaps very little) resonant attuning to survive. The memory of that

THE PSYCHOBIOSPIRITUAL PERSON

This figure shows you our conceptualization of who we are, our human personhood.

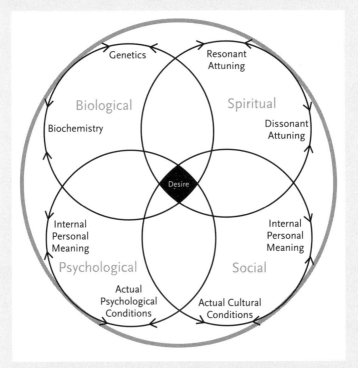

Human beings have four aspects: a biological aspect that includes our genetic endowment and our biochemistry, a psychological aspect that includes the actual psychological conditions in which we live and the internal personal meanings we make of those conditions, a social aspect that includes our actual cultural conditions and the internal personal meanings we make of them, and a spiritual aspect that includes both resonant and dissonant attuning.

experience—perhaps with a loving grandparent, aunt, or babysitter —no matter how brief, remains in the brain. The neural pathways created in those life-giving moments can continue to exist throughout our lives even without constant reinforcement. This means that a child who has experienced some brief measure of resonant attuning—despite an ongoing environment of emotional, physical, and spiritual deprivation—can have a rich and full life. If you survived a painful, neglectful childhood, somehow you received enough resonant attuning to make it possible for you to live. That does not mean, of course, that you have no scars or pain from that difficult experience, but neither does it mean you are closed off from the possibility of restoration and hope.

Our deliberate placement of resonant and dissonant attuning in our spiritual aspect of human personhood rather than in our brain or in our psyche reaps the benefit of bringing the soul back into our conceptualization of human personhood. Even though in modern times the human psyche is equated to the "mind," the ancient Greeks considered psyche to be the "soul." Webster defines *soul* as "the spiritual principle embodied in human beings." Thus by using *soul* in the sense of our spiritual aspect of personhood, we reclaim the original Greek meaning of psyche and move out of mind/body dualism.

At our core is sacred Desire, our urge to be one with the Divine. It flows through the arrows that represent the mutual interactive exchange of information and energy among our various aspects. This multidirectional flow of attuning—within our self, between us and others, and between us and the Divine—influences how our brains develop, how our minds develop, and how our bodies function. It determines who we are and what we do. A change in any one aspect changes all of who we are.

Source: Nancy K. Morrison and Sally K. Severino, "The Biology of Morality," *Zygon: Journal of Religion and Science* 38 (2003): 855–69.

The power of resonant attuning, so clearly revealed in the loving gaze between mother and infant, continues to shape and influence us throughout our lives. In our next chapter, we'll see how attuning changes as an infant becomes a toddler, a time when the child discovers a larger world and parents face the necessity of setting boundaries and limits on their child's behavior.

CHAPTER 3

THE WIDENING BOUNDARIES OF LIFE AND LOVE

> [T]he moment I stepped into the house I felt a trembling along my skin. . . . The body knows things a long time before the mind catches up to them.
>
> —FOURTEEN-YEAR-OLD LILLY, IN *The Secret Life of Bees*

THE TREMBLING ALONG HER SKIN that Lilly feels is what scientists call *neuroception*.[1] Neuroception—the processing of information from the environment through our senses—is the way we determine whether people or places are safe, dangerous, or life-threatening. We propose that when our mirror neurons attune us to another person, our neuroception system—programmed into the DNA of our genes—is encountering the neuroception system of the other. In that encounter we get an immediate felt body experience of the other person. Our first knowing is a nonverbal somatic knowing. Only later does our mind catch up, bringing with it a cognitive understanding of what our body knows.

Earlier we talked about the first year of life when preverbal somatic knowing—neuroception—prevails. During this time the attuning of infant and caregivers creates what neuroscientist Vittorio Gallese calls a "we-centric" space and what we authors call a second womb of compassion.[2] Unlike the physical womb, which is inherently compassionate in the sense that the baby's needs are met without much effort on baby's part, the "we-centric" space is a compassionate womb only to the extent that infant and caregivers co-create it with love. In the we-centric womb, the infant takes the vital information (sensations, states of mind, his very *being*) and energy (physical, emotional, spiritual) that he co-creates with another, and he begins building these experiences into basic trust or mistrust of self, other, and sacred Desire. Optimally, in the first year, resonant attuning between infant and caregivers predominates, laying the foundation in our brains for trust.

During the second year of life, infants become toddlers who

NEUROCEPTION

Neuroception, a term coined by psychologist Stephen Porges, is the way we distinguish whether people or places are safe, dangerous, or life threatening. Neuroception automatically, without our conscious awareness, triggers neurobiologically determined behaviors that will draw us either to or away from people or places.

The behaviors that defend us from people or places (fight/flight or freeze) are more primitive. They take place in the older parts of our brain—the brain stem and the dorsal vagus nerve. Human beings have newer neural systems—our cortex and the ventral vagus nerve—that support prosocial behavior. This means that for us to engage with others, we must assess safety and then shut off the fight/flight or freeze reactions in safe places.

Faulty neuroception "may include a person's inability to *inhibit* defense systems in a safe environment or the inability to *activate* defense systems in a risky environment—or both."

Source: Stephen W. Porges, "Neuroception: A Subconscious System for Detecting Threats and Safety," *Zero to Three* (May 2004): 20.

begin walking and talking. Now socialization must increase the wisdom of body, mind, and spirit for continuing growth of the toddler in community.[3] An important avenue for this growth (social, spiritual, biological, and moral) is a different kind of attuning that we call *dissonant attuning*. Dissonant attuning is connecting with another in disharmony.

Take seventeen-month-old Susie and her mother, for example. Susie runs exuberantly into the street from the front yard where she has been playing. Mother, seeing Susie's potential danger, ceases to be in sync with Susie's enthusiasm. Filled with fear, Mother screams, "No!" Susie, drunk with the glee of running into space and expecting a comparable response from Mother (a resonantly attuned elation), instead hears an unanticipated thwart (a dissonantly attuned disappointment). Mother, in harmony with Susie's danger, meets Susie's glee with disharmony. This dissonant attuning experience triggers a shock-like reaction in Susie.

Susie stops in her tracks as her brain neuroception system automatically says, "Danger, slow down, assess!" Physiologically she is in a fear-based state. Being human, her mind eventually catches up to her body; and when it does, her awareness splits—one part experiences herself as small and disapproved and another part experiences her mother as large and disapproving. This is how dissonant attuning leaves us—as it did Susie—in a split internal state.

What happens next is crucial. Mother runs and snatches Susie into her arms and kisses her as she explains, "You must not run into the street; it's dangerous." In the "we-centric" womb of compassion, Mother both dissonantly disapproved of Susie's dangerous behavior and also, by hugging and kissing her, resonantly attuned to Susie's painful state of experiencing disapproval. Implicitly she invited Susie to understand that "no" reflects neither bad Susie nor bad mothering but Susie's growth and her mother's appropriate new expectations of her daughter. This is healthy, nontraumatic dissonant attuning at its best, where Mother uses dissonant attuning to stop Susie's behavior and resonant attuning to repair Susie's inner split state, bringing her back into harmony.

Such dissonant attuning is a valuable tool that tells us when we are out of sync with another. Used by mother, father, or other caregiver, it stimulates a child's growth. It encourages a capacity for learning from and repairing the unavoidable dissonant attuning experiences that we all encounter in life. It becomes the template for knowing when we are out of sync with our sacred Desire and the template for knowing how we can get back into harmony with it.

The danger in dissonant attuning occurs when the dissonance is not repaired and the child is left in a state of fear. This is how we are taught to mistrust our sacred Desire and to hate others. Lieutenant Joe expresses it well in Rogers and Hammerstein's musical *South Pacific* when he sings:

> You've got to be taught to hate and fear.
> You've got to be taught from year to year.
> It's got to be drummed in your dear little ear.
> You've got to be carefully taught.
>
> You've got to be taught to be afraid
> Of people whose eyes are oddly made
> And people whose skin is a diff'rent shade,
> You've got to be carefully taught.
>
> You've got to be taught before it's too late,
> Before you are six or seven or eight,
> To hate all the people your relatives hate.
> You've got to be carefully taught!
> You've got to be carefully taught!

While unrepaired dissonant attuning experiences leave us in a physiology of fear, repaired dissonant attuning together with resonant attuning experiences foster empathy, which is awareness of

THE POLYVAGAL SYSTEM: REGULATION OF SOCIAL ENGAGEMENT

The polyvagal system is at work in neuroception. It involves the vagus nerve—the "wandering nerve" that we read about in chapter 2. The Polyvagal Theory describes three stages in the development of a mammal's autonomic nervous system.

Stage	Character	Physiology	Behavior
I	Primitive unmyelinated parasympathetic Dorsal vagus	Depresses metabolic activity	Freezing
II	Sympathetic nervous system	Increases metabolic activity Inhibits primitive Vagus	Fight or flight
III	Myelinated parasympathetic Ventral vagus	Regulates cardiac output to foster engagement with the environment	Social communication

We understand Porges' stages in development of the vagus nerve to translate into the following three states—two produced by dissonant attuning and one produced by resonant attuning.

Dissonant attuning puts us in two fear-filled states. First, it automatically elicits a startle reaction:

- The sympathetic component of the autonomic nervous system is activated.
- Heart rate increases, blood pressure elevates, respiration increases, and muscle tone increases.

This is a hyperaroused state with hypervigilance.

Sidebar continues

The Polyvagal System, *continued*

Second, a later-forming reaction is that of numbing:

- The dorsal vagal primitive parasympathetic system is aroused.
- Heart rate decreases, blood pressure drops, respirations decrease, and muscle tone decreases.
- The person disengages from the external world.

Resonant attuning puts us in a state of perceived safety:

- The ventral vagal parasympathetic system, unique to mammals, is activated.
- Social communication results.

Sources: Stephen W. Porges, "The Polyvagal Theory: Phylogenetic Substrates of a Social Nervous System," *International Journal of Psychophysiology* 42 (2001): 123–46; Stephen W. Porges, "Neuroception: A Subconscious System for Detecting Threats and Safety," *Zero to Three* (May 2004): 19–24; Allan N. Schore, *Affect Dysregulation and Disorders of the Self* (New York: W. W. Norton, 2003).

attuning, or "mindsight."[4] Empathy is realizing that we are experiencing another's feelings. Through our mirror neurons, we are bodily identifying with the other's state of being. Empathy is reciprocity, valuing and respecting one another's feelings, and recognizing that both have the same and different feelings. It is this "tender cooperation" that is the foundation of all morality.

Both resonant and dissonant attuning experiences are necessary for the development of sacred Desire. Resonant attuning awakens us to love; dissonant attuning informs us that we are out of sync with another or with our Desire. Dissonant attuning produces the wish to return to a state of harmony, and it requires resonant attuning to do so. Our life experiences are thus training our brains to assess safety (situations where resonant attuning prevails) and risk (situations where dissonant attuning prevails). Pediatrician and psychiatrist Stanley Greenspan tells us two clinical vignettes about the same child, Cara. From our perspective, the first vignette shows us a relationship of dissonant attuning, and the second shows us resonant attuning that repairs dissonant attuning. The following vignettes allow us to see Cara's emotional and behavioral responses to the two different kinds of attuning.

A mother took her twelve-month-old daughter, Cara, to a psychologist for evaluation because she did not babble like other children her age. Cara underwent two examinations. Her first evaluation was by an examiner who focused on the task of testing. The examiner wanted Cara to cooperate with his test and was not attuning to her needs. Cara, experiencing his insistence as his being out of harmony with her subjectivity, refused to cooperate with him.

> The child sits on her mother's lap at a table, staring defiance at a psychologist who holds out a scarlet peg and motions toward a bright blue board. Won't you put it in a hole, he asks encouragingly. Won't you try, her mother cajoles. Cara . . . grabs the peg and hurls it to the floor.. . .
>
> [The] second examiner took a different approach with Cara. He first watched her playing by herself and saw an active, eager explorer. She [Cara] listened to the sound of toy cars crashing, examined a rubber ball's rough surface, tried to yank on her mother's nose. At the examiner's suggestion, the mother permitted the pull and responded, "Toot toot!" Cara smiled and pulled again. This time "Oop shoop!" greeted her effort, bringing a bigger smile. Then Mom gestured for Cara to offer her own nose for pulling. The delighted child thrust out her scrunched, beaming face. Mother gently squeezed and, to her astonishment, heard her joyful daughter utter "Mo mo." These contributions to the game were Cara's very first distinct sound.[5]

This examiner creates a "we-centric" womb of compassion,

The Biology and Physiology of Human Relationships

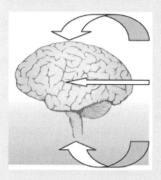

Human cortex (personhood brain)
Mediation of attuning
Mirror neurons
Limbic system (emotional brain)
Biochemistry of attachment
Oxytocin and Vasopressin
Brain stem (instinctual brain)
Autonomic regulation of social engagement, neuroception
Vagal system

Human cortex: Mirror neurons appear to mediate attuning between infant and caregivers. Resonant attuning gives rise to imitation, identification, and empathy, which enables members of a group to recognize one another. Eventually, the child's increasing capacity for embodied simulation of the other gives rise to thinking.

Limbic system: Monitors the external world and the internal bodily environment and orchestrates their congruence. The amygdala has a direct connection to the brain-stem vagal system, and it reaches up to the frontal cortex to change our thinking accordingly. Increased love leads to increased oxytocin, increased ventral vagal activity, and social engagement with others. Increased fear leads to decreased oxytocin and either sympathetic nervous system fight/flight reactions or parasympathetic numbing reactions.

Brain stem: Regulates vital bodily functions (heart rate, blood pressure, respiration, body temperature, digestion) and reflexes (sneezing, coughing, vomiting, neuroception).

Sources: Vittorio Gallese, "The Manifold Nature of Interpersonal Relations: The Quest for a Common Mechanism," *Philosophical Transactions of the Royal Society of London*, 358 (2003): 517–28; Thomas Lewis, Fari Amini, and Richard Lannon, *A General Theory of Love* (New York: Random House, 2000).

where he cooperates tenderly with both Cara's and also Mother's needs. He understands that Cara's reaching out for her mother's nose is a playful attempt to engage Mother. He encourages Mother to attune resonantly to Cara by letting Cara pull her nose and by responding "toot-toot." Within his resonant attuning, Mother could follow the examiner's suggestions and Cara could move from defiance to cooperation. With examiner and Mother resonantly attuning to her core essence, Cara could name Mother—"Mo mo." She could utter those words only within resonant attuning.

The good news is that our attuning keeps us connected in a network of relationships that is mutually constructed and mutually growth-promoting. The bad news, as we mentioned earlier, is that dissonant attuning can be a stumbling block to the growth of our self, our relationships, and our Desire. It becomes a stumbling block when it is left unrepaired or when it is traumatic, such as occurs with physical, emotional, and/or sexual abuse. In all of these instances, seeds are sewn for mistrust of others. Mistrust of others becomes the template for mistrust of our sacred Desire.

Cara seemed to suffer from unrepaired dissonant attuning. All we are told in the vignette is that Cara's mother attempted to require expected behaviors of her child—in one instance babbling and in another putting a peg in the hole. Mother's preset expectations created dissonant attuning to Cara's current needs. This dissonant attuning created a stumbling block to the freedom of creativity between the two of them. This creativity could happen only when Cara's mother could resonantly attune to her.

The first examiner's focus on the task instead of on Cara added more dissonant attuning and furthered Cara's refusal to cooperate. Cara could not get out of her defiance without the help of resonant attuning. Mother could not get out of her preset expectations on her own. By resonantly attuning to Cara and to her mother, the second examiner moved both of them away from the nontraumatic unrepaired dissonant attuning that blocked their growth. Once Cara and her mother moved into resonant attuning, the natural flow of sacred Desire was set free to be expressed in those joyful "toot toots" and "Mo mos."

Dissonant attuning in and of itself is not traumatic. Trauma occurs in two ways. It occurs when chronic, repeated dissonant attuning goes unrepaired. It also occurs when dissonant attuning overwhelms our usual coping mechanisms and is perceived as life-threatening, such as what happens in physical, sexual, or emotional abuse. This second type of dissonant attuning is inherently traumatic. It creates alternating physiological states of hyperarousal and numbing, both of which are states based in fear. As we begin to live more persistently in these states, they lead us to misread environmental cues as dangerous or as safe even when they are not. As a result we live out of sync with our environment and out of sync with our sacred Desire. Our actions express—not the creative urge within us—but an urge distorted by fear. This is suggested in Cara's behavior with the first examiner.

Stanley Greenspan also offers us another example of such distortion.[6]

> [Baby] Emma embarks on her own cautious explorations. Extremely
> sensitive to sound, she nonetheless begins experimenting with
> her own voice, and one day, babbling excitedly, she also boldly tries
> to explore Mom's nose with her fingers. But her mother becomes
> tense when Emma grows inquisitive and fears that the childish
> overtures are a sign of inappropriate aggression rather than simply
> assertiveness.

Mother does not resonantly attune to Emma's inquisitiveness. Her fear-based evaluations lead her to perceive aggression when, in fact, it is not present. This prevents her from correctly attuning to what is pleasurable exploration and leads her into controlling what she perceives to be Emma's aggression.

> She pokes back at Emma's nose and drowns out the infant's pro-
> tests with admonitions that "touching people's faces isn't nice." This

pattern is repeated in numerous ways every time Emma is assertive. Before Emma has reached ten months, she has learned the risks of expressing herself. She gradually abandons exploration [her Desire's spontaneous expression] in favor of whining, displaying increased passivity in the face of her fear.

This behavior reflects a distortion of her Desire. If resonant attuning does not transform her fear, she remains at risk of becoming increasingly passive.

Later on, when bolder children pick on her, this bright and dutiful child may well blame herself, remaining all the while passive, insecure, and easily frightened. She may even choose domineering friends who can lead her around.[7]

This example is not meant to frighten us but to encourage us to live as heroically as possible. Though we, by ourselves, cannot undo fears that distort the expression of our sacred Desire, we are not impotent. We can seek out relationships that provide resonant attuning and thus help repair our states of dissonant attuning.

In addition, we can live with an attitude of contrition motivated by sorrow about the times we live from distorted Desire. This means humbly accepting our fear-driven behavior as the best we could do at that particular moment, all things considered. As long as we are not making an excuse and thereby not trying to fix what is changeable, our best is good enough at that time for us to live heroically. Humbly accepting the upset we feel when our distorted Desire meets another's distorted Desire can help bring a state of trauma into a state of resonant attuning that is ultimately reparative.

In the next chapter we will talk more about living in harmony with our sacred Desire.

CHAPTER 4

LIVING IN SACRED DESIRE

Though Eden is lost
its loveliness
remains in the heart
and the imagination.

—MARY OLIVER, "FIREFLIES"

DESIRE URGES US into relationship, but it requires being received by another. Until we enter an encounter where resonant attuning is possible, it remains a potential. When our sacred Desire is met with resonant attuning, we come into the fullness of our being and experience joy, which fuels our Desire for even more relational experience.

Given the best of circumstances during the first eighteen months of human life, infant-caregiver relationships activate—to use Mary Oliver's words—the "loveliness" of goodness in our "heart and the imagination." When caregivers receive us with resonant attuning, they certainly activate a physiology in our brains that we experience as goodness. Their resonant attuning—with experiences of love, comfort, and joy—structures our right cortex. This early resonant attuning can be understood as the human experience of the Garden of Eden. We carry this experience with us throughout our lives. It forms the foundation that each of us revisits and builds upon for our own expressions of love, trust, and goodness.

An essential ingredient in transmitting love to infants is what psychiatrist Daniel J. Siegel calls "feeling felt."[1] "Feeling felt" is the deep wordless experience when another senses what we need and gives us an unmistakable confirming response. This might be as simple as a baby crying when hungry or soiled and a mother responding by feeding or changing a diaper, or as complex as an adult reading a facial expression of delight when a baby smiles and responding with a joyous smile.

We are proposing that "feeling felt" involves resonant attuning and is mediated by the mirror neurons of both mother and infant. The brains of both are engaged and changed in the "we-centric" space in a process such as this: When the infant's face expresses his feelings, Mother's mirror neurons are activated as if she were feeling the same emotions. Her embodied experience now gets expressed on her face and is reflected back to the infant. Seeing this emotional confirmation of his feelings, the infant knows on his deepest level that he is known within his mother's deepest level. He "feels felt."

Mother is also creating an interpersonal relationship in which the infant feels that he is valued and valuable to Mother. Mother also feels valuable and valued. In resonant attuning, feeling valued and valuable are inextricably intertwined.

The idea that we are literally living the experience of the other through resonant attuning builds on a wealth of scientific studies that show how our early interpersonal relationships biologically structure our brain. Studies include the work in the 1940s of Anna Freud, who showed the importance of parent-infant bonding, and also the work of Rene Spitz, cited in chapter 2. Carrying these efforts forward, British medical doctor and psychoanalyst John Bowlby launched our understanding of how our attachment bonds to caregivers—laid down in our brain circuits—become the means by which we bond to one another throughout life.

Following in Bowlby's footsteps, his associate Mary Ainsworth

ATTACHMENT PATTERNS

Summary of Findings from Attachment Research

Parenting Behavior	Child's Strange Situation Test	Adult Attachment Interview
Autonomous: Emotionally available, perceptive, and effective	Secure Attachment: Child shows distress when mother leaves but is comforted by reunion, returns to play	Detailed memory, balanced perspective, coherent autobiographical narrative
Dismissing: Emotionally distant and rejecting	Insecure-Avoidant Attachment: Child exhibits no overt distress at mother's leaving and on her returning does not seek to be near her, appears to play uninterrupted	Remembers little of the past and what is recalled is emotionally bland, dismisses the importance of interpersonal relationships
Enmeshed-Ambivalent: Inconsistent emotional availability	Insecure-Resistant Attachment: Child exhibits distress even prior to mother's leaving and on her returning is difficult to sooth, doesn't play	Excessive verbal output, still caught up in unresolved negative emotions, incoherent autobiographical narrative
Disorganized: Disorienting or frightening	Disorganized-Disoriented Attachment: Child is frightened by mother's leaving but on her return, he exhibits contradictory attachment behaviors, e.g., when he rises at mother's return, fear overwhelms him and he falls prone on the floor	Disorganized and confusing autobiographical narrative

Attachment research shows us several things:

1. The adults' ways of thinking about their own childhoods influence their way of relating to their infant.
2. The child's relatedness to mother and father shapes the way the child relates to others.

invented a videotaped reproducible laboratory procedure called the Strange Situation Test. This test allowed her to classify twelve- to twenty-month-old babies according to one of three attachment patterns: secure (discussed in this chapter), insecure, or disorganized/disoriented (discussed in the next chapter). These attachment patterns are the internal working models that babies build into their brains of themselves, their caregivers, and their relationships.

A student of Ainsworth, Mary Main, extended this work by developing the Adult Attachment Interview. The interview leads to the classification of parents into attachment patterns that both reflect how the adult bonded with his or her parents in the past and also predict how the adult will bond with his or her own children in the present or in the future (see "Attachment Patterns").

Parents and infants whose brains have been shaped within resonant attuning form secure attachment bonds. Secure attachment patterns characterize 55 percent of young adult American relationships.[2] These individuals trust that key people in their lives will be available and supportive in times of need. They view the world as an emotionally secure place and life's problems as

---

3. Personal relationships shape thinking and behaviors throughout life.

Sources: Mary D. S. Ainsworth, M. C. Blehar, E. Waters, and S. Wall, *Patterns of Attachment: A Psychological Study of the Strange Situation* (Hillsdale, NJ: Lawrence Erlbaum, 1978); John Bowlby, *Attachment* (New York: Basic Books, 1969); Erik Hesse, "The Adult Attachment Interview: Historical and Current Perspectives," in *Handbook of Attachment: Theory, Research, and Clinical Applications,* ed. J. Cassidy and P. Shaver (New York: Guilford, 1999), 395–433; Erik Hesse and Mary Main, "Second-Generation Effects of Unresolved Trauma as Observed in Non-Maltreating Parents: Dissociated, Frightened and Threatening Parental Behavior," *Psychoanalytic Inquiry* 19 (1999): 481–540; Erik Hesse and Mary Main, "Disorganized Infant, Child, and Adult Attachment: Collapse in Behavioral and Attentional Strategies," *Journal of the American Psychoanalytic Association* 48, no. 4 (2000): 1097–1127.

manageable. Their self-esteem is reasonably high and is maintained relatively easily. They have great freedom to give their attention to work and play.

In daily life we instantly recognize these people. I (Nancy) vividly remember such a person. I had just completed chemotherapy and radiation therapy for breast cancer. Physically and emotionally exhausted, I traveled to the motherhouse of the Sisters of Charity of Leavenworth, Kansas, to visit my spiritual mentor, Sister Mary Aloys. One day, while Sister Mary Aloys was at work, I ventured to the post office on the small liberal arts college campus nearby that was run by the Sisters.

As I purchased a postage stamp from the tiny woman at the window, I felt her seeing me. Her gaze of saintly love filled me with awe. "Will that be all?"

Her peace-filled voice moved me to tears of joy. I sensed that she was completely and lovingly present to me.

When I mentioned the experience to Sister Mary Aloys, she knew immediately not only who the person was, but also what the experience had been. This physically teeny woman characteristically met people with love, received their Desire to relate, and responded in a way uniquely appropriate for the encounter. She could do so, Sister Mary Aloys said, "because she accepted who she was created to be. She accepted that she was created good."

What do we mean by "good"? Some might find the definition in the community established by Thich ("Venerable") Nhat Hahn. The community is called the Order of Interbeing. Through their Buddhist practice, the practitioner-activists living there become aware of the interconnectedness of us all. This awareness leads them to altruistic efforts where they work to alleviate the suffering of refugees, political prisoners, and starving people in Vietnam and other economically poor countries around the world.

Others might find the definition of good within Islam. While it is not one of Islam's five pillars, Muslims would agree that they have a duty to enjoin the good both as individuals and also to help others do so. This duty applies to the family and to society. Islamic jurist and scholar Dr. Khaled Abou El Fadl defines good Muslims as ones who "honor their neighbors, feel for and help the poor, speak the truth, keep their promises, abstain from consuming alcoholic beverages, and refrain from committing adultery, fornicating, cheating, or stealing."[3]

In the Christian tradition Jesus defines "good" in the parable of the Good Samaritan.

> A man was going down from Jerusalem to Jericho, and fell into the hands of robbers, who stripped him, beat him, and went away, leaving him half dead. Now by chance a priest was going down that road; and when he saw him, he passed by on the other side. So likewise a Levite, when he came to the place and saw him, passed by on the other side. But a Samaritan while traveling came near him; and when he saw him, he was moved with pity. He went to him and bandaged his wounds, having poured oil and wine on them. Then he put him on his own animal, brought him to an inn, and took care of him. The next day he took out two denarii, gave them to the innkeeper, and said, "Take care of him; and when I come back, I will repay you whatever more you spend."[4]

"Good" is the Samaritan who saw. What he saw produced in his body an emotional experience of the subjective reality of the man in the ditch. The Samaritan sensed what fit. "Good" was his being uniquely appropriate for the situation. He dared to be loving by forming a personal relationship.

Is this not resonant attuning? When we see and hear with an unclouded attraction to the true experience of the other, then we can give a response that fits the other's call.

In this instance "good" happened between enemies. The story of the Good Samaritan, a social outcast, would have created a scandal in the minds of Jesus' listeners on hearing that the Samaritan did the unexpected. The Samaritan was not expected to feel compassion and to stop and help the injured man. The wounded man's fellow Jews—the priest and the Levite—would have been expected to do so. Both were religious men who were familiar with the laws of ethics. But they passed the wounded man by. Instead, the outcast stopped to help a man who in any other circumstances would not have wanted to be touched by him.

The Samaritan acted from what we call a primary incentive for good.[5] A primary incentive for good is our primary wish to be good in order to bring pleasure to another and experience pleasure with another. This unclouded attraction to what is good arises from our sacred Desire. Medieval philosophers endorsed this idea when they defined "good" as that which the will always desires.[6]

By acting out of his sacred Desire's primary incentive for good, the Samaritan listened to what his body told him and knew the truth of what he was called to do. He honored his connection to the injured man and a relationship came to life through the exercise of the Samaritan's freedom to respond to a call from someone in need. The Samaritan's act and the injured man's response show us that all of us are connected and we are one community.

It is our human nature to attune resonantly to one another in ways that reflect our uniqueness of being. C. S. Lewis clearly illustrates this in his *Narnia* series. Lewis imagined the four children hearing for the first time in the beavers' den the name of Aslan, who, in the story, is the epitome of good. Each child sensed the name differently depending on his or her temperament, age, and background, although each was resonantly attuning.

> At the name of Aslan each one of the children felt something jump in its inside. Edmund felt a sensation of mysterious horror. Peter felt suddenly brave and adventurous. Susan felt as if some delicious smell or some delightful strain of music had just floated by her. And Lucy got the feeling you have when you wake up in the morning and

realize that it is the beginning of the holidays, or the beginning of summer.[7]

How each child responded to the name of Aslan and how we respond to life's challenges depends on our attuning to an inner essence that "jumps" inside our bodies. Then, we must respond "yes" or "no" to the call of good. When we respond with "yes," we stand in awe of the reality that we creatures are capable of experiencing resonant attuning.

We propose that resonant attuning is not just minds affecting minds and spirits touching spirits, but also bodies influencing bodies through mirror neurons. Research has shown that when one person physically touches another person, electromagnetic energy flows from his heart to the brain of the person who is touched. The heart pattern of the touching person is transmitted to the brain of the person who is touched. The brain waves of the person touched synchronize with the heart rhythm of the person touching. This has been documented by comparing the electroencephalogram of the one touched with the electrocardiogram of the one doing the touching. Our hearts literally affect the brains of those around us.[8]

Responding "yes" to the call of good not only affects our hearts and brains, it also affects us morally. Our morality—our ability to determine the "rightness" or "wrongness" of our actions—is based not only on following certain rules, but also on knowing the impact of our actions on another, which we know through attuning. When we are resonantly attuning, our morality expresses valuing based in love.[9] We consider this condition of living from our goodness to be our First Nature because the template for our First Nature is laid down in our right brain during the first months of life.

First Nature is our growth into goodness. Growth begins when we attune to another in resonance, resulting biologically in the

FIRST NATURE

When our sacred Desire is met with resonant attuning, we grow in goodness, we act in goodness, we view the world as fundamentally good, and we morally value life. We grow into wholeness as the diagram below illustrates.

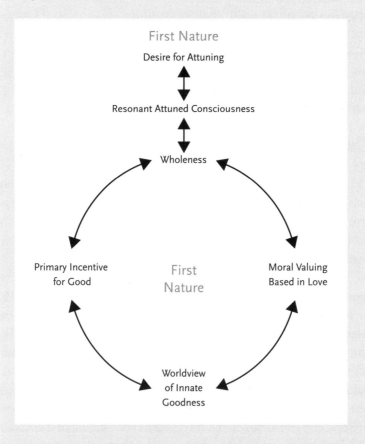

Source: Nancy K. Morrison and Sally K. Severino, "The Biology of Morality," *Zygon: Journal of Religion and Science* 38, no. 4 (2003): 855–69.

activation of the parasympathetic ventral vagal system (autonomic nervous system) and stimulation of the release of oxytocin (hormone in blood stream and neurotransmitter in brain), our body's system for calm and connection. Psychologically, this results in establishing secure attachments with others where our minds can tell coherent autobiographical narratives about our psychological and social circumstances. Spiritually, this results in the experience of loving and being loved (see "First Nature").

The Samaritan exemplified living in First Nature. He expressed love when he valued the half-dead Jew. His response reflected his resonant attuning both to his own essential goodness and also to the goodness of the stranger. This created a mutual belonging between the two strangers.[10] Their belonging together came from love.

Living in our First Nature, where we experience life as good and our being as loving, establishes in us a worldview based on four convictions. First, we feel that goodness, healthy and constructive needs, and striving to love are primary. These qualities exist from the beginning of time. Second, we understand that violence is a reaction to the frustration of our sacred Desire for harmony. Third, we believe that violence neither fixes things nor restores us. Instead, violence creates more violence. And fourth, we feel that violence need not be expressed as such but can be managed within our relationships by being recognized, owned, and repaired. This occurs through acceptance of the violence we personally feel, through inner transformation of that violence by love, and (where possible) through reparation of our frustrating relationships that elicited it.[11]

The view of the world and us as good—not as battered by our fears or made impotent by our limitations—frees us to live from our sacred Desire. What is at the core of the parable of the Good Samaritan is his freedom to choose what gifts to give and to whom based on his resonant attuning to the call of the Jew who needed the goodness of the Samaritan. The Samaritan acts primarily not to save the Jew or to give him medical attention or food, but to

THE SCIENCE OF FIRST NATURE

At least two groups of researchers in the United States have studied human beings in their First Nature.

One group is that of the late psychiatrist Eugene d'Aquili and radiologist Andrew Newberg at the University of Pennsylvania Medical School. They studied SPECT (single photon emission computerized tomography) scans of brains of American Buddhists practicing Tibetan meditation and Franciscan nuns engaged in contemplative prayer. When the monks and nuns reached a state of transcendence, their brain scans showed increased activity in the attention association area, situated in the prefrontal cortex and richly interconnected with the limbic system, and decreased activity in the orientation association area. Also, the right side of their brain was more active than the left. The nuns described their experiences as that of immanent divine presence, of absolute unity or wholeness, or of empty divine reality, and of the self dissolving into a great unity. The monks reported a state of ecstasy and peace in which they felt completely loved and completely loving.

A second group is that of Richard Davidson, professor of psychology and psychiatry at the University of Wisconsin at Madison. His group studied, in depth, one Tibetan monk who had trained for more than three decades in the Himalayas to practice meditation. By using two different EEG (electroencephalogram) caps, one with 128 sensors and one with 256, they monitored the monk's brain during six meditative states. Each state showed distinct differences in brain-wave patterns. In the state of generating compassion there was a dramatic increase in electrical activity in that portion of the monk's prefrontal cortex that previous research has identified as a locus for positive emotions.

These findings lend support to the importance of our prefrontal cortex for mediating our spirit's attuning.

Sources: Eugene d'Aquili and Andrew Newberg, *The Mystical Mind: Probing the Biology of Religious Experience* (Minneapolis: Fortress, 1999); Daniel Goleman, *Destructive Emotions* (New York: Bantam Books, 2003).

express his Desire to give freely and to express his goodness. Just like the Samaritan, we are most imaginative and creative when we are most in touch with our sacred Desire. Then, we are in the flow of life's creative energy that flows out of us when it is called forth by another.

In our next chapter, we will look at what happens to us when our sacred Desire gets distorted.

CHAPTER 5

THE DISTORTION OF DESIRE

Each one of us possesses a Holy Spark, but not
every one exhibits it to the best advantage.

—RABBI ISRAEL OF RIZIN

OUR DEEPEST BIOLOGICAL imperative is to form attachment
bonds with our important caregivers. This imperative is
expressed through attuning. Our ability to attune is a magnificent
gift. It is our strength, but it can also be our weakness. It is our
strength when our important caregivers meet us with resonant
attuning. Then we form secure attachment patterns and when
something frightens us, we can go to our safe caregivers who
calm us. Calming keeps our sacred Desire undistorted, letting us
exhibit our "Holy Spark" to best advantage.

Our ability to attune becomes our weakness when our important caregivers meet us with traumatic or with dissonant attuning
that goes unrepaired. Then, our source of security becomes our
source of alarm.[1] This thrusts us into a dilemma where our biology forces us to go for comfort to the person who is frightening
or threatening us. The dilemma is: How do we make our abusive
father or neglecting mother our source of soothing?

We must attach to an abusive parent—especially when we're
infants—because it is the only way we can survive. We yearn to
restore whatever resonant attuning we may have experienced.
It is our only connection to good. Even in a fear-based state, we
cling to a hope for goodness. But as long as the dissonant attuning

remains unrepaired, we never actually become unafraid. Instead we become split within our self—split between our fear and our need for security. Because our primary need for safety and our primary Desire for resonant attuning are augmented by fear, we must find compromises that allow us to stay attached to our essential but frightening caregiver.

We call these compromises secondary incentives for good.[2] They are the ways we try to *do* good in order to avoid losing the potential for resonant attuning. We develop these behaviors to preserve and to stay in relationship with those we need but who are dissonantly attuning to us. Others have called these behaviors "defense mechanisms," "habitual behaviors," and "personality strategies." We prefer naming them "secondary incentives for good" to emphasize that human beings, even when our Desire is distorted, yearn to *be* good and to restore resonant attuning with the people whom we absolutely need.

We italicized *do* and *be* in the previous paragraph to highlight that these are different ways we respond to others deriving from different states that we live in. When—as in the previous chapter—we live in our First Nature, which is based in a physiology of love, we can *be* more spontaneous and express our sacred Desire free from fear. We express it in an unclouded attraction to good, a primary incentive for good.

In this chapter, however, we are describing a different state that we live in, a fear-based state that splits our awareness and distorts our Desire. Our Holy Spark is not exhibited to best advantage. Our attraction to good is clouded by fear, and what we *do* is compromised. These compromised behaviors, these secondary incentives for good, are our attempts to stay in relationships when we can't spontaneously *be*. We can't express our sacred Desire free from fear.

Secondary incentives for good get laid down in our brains as neural networks and are expressed in our behaviors as forms of insecure or disorganized/disoriented attachment patterns. When we live out these attachment patterns, we overestimate the danger-ousness of unknown others and deny the danger of our in-group to whom we must cling. We tell ourselves that we're not afraid of our mother or father; we're afraid of those other "bad" people. Because we fear them, we have little empathy with strangers. We maintain our self-esteem by emphasizing the superior worth of our in-group and by tearing down other groups. Such self-esteem is tenuous, leaving us very little freedom in our work or our play. We not only shy away from those "bad" people; we also shy away from new ideas.

When we live in relationships that are maintained by insecure and disorganized/disoriented attachment bonds that distort our Desire, we act out of a love distorted by fear. We may fear losing the person who threatens us. We may fear losing that person's love or approval. We may fear punishment by that person. In order to feel acceptable, we may establish unrealistic ideals, which we then fear we may not live up to. Whatever the form of our fear, we develop fear-based behaviors in our attempt to cope with threat-ening people who cause us anxiety, shame, helplessness, and despair, but whom we nonetheless need.

Fear-based behaviors become problematic when we use them excessively and lock ourselves into rigid reactions. These reactions get established in our brain as information that is not integrated with our other knowledge. It is as though a bunch of neurons form a circuit where the original threat (the dissonant attuning)—com-plete with image, emotion, and negative self-assessment—is closed off in an attempt to diminish the pain by keeping the pain out of awareness both within us and between others and us.

This maneuver is essential because we can't give up the pos-sibility of resonant attuning. But it creates an illusion of good-ness that distorts our spontaneous *being* into more rigid patterns of *doing* and prevents us from living in touch with our sacred Desire. This illusion covers up the very alive overwhelming and unrepaired dissonant attuning that caused and continues to cause our fear-based behaviors. By walling off unacceptable parts of our relationships and ourselves, we feel in control of our pain, but the walled-off elements continue to distort our Desire, to obscure our Holy Spark, and to determine our perceptions and understandings of life. Once this happens we are no longer living in our First Nature. Instead, we are living in our Second Nature.

Growth into our Second Nature begins when we attune to others in dissonance, resulting biologically in the activation of the sympathetic nervous system (autonomic nervous system) and stimulation of the release of vasopressin (hormone) plus adrenaline and noradrenalin (neurotransmitters), our body's system for fight or flight. Psychologically this results in establishing insecure or disorganized/disoriented attachments to others where our minds cannot tell coherent autobiographical narratives about our psychological and social circumstances. Spiritually this results in the experience of wanting to feel powerful and wanting control over life ("Second Nature," page 50).

In our Second Nature, which is the product of being locked into secondary incentives for good, we unwittingly cause harm because our freedom to choose how and to whom we respond has been perverted by our fear. In our Second Nature, the distortion of our Desire distorts our perception. We are convinced that we're doing what is good even when our behavior is destructive.

Let us return to the story of the Good Samaritan and see how Second Nature is revealed in it. In this story the priest and the Levite lived in their Second Nature. They did not freely respond to the call from the poor man who fell among thieves and lay by the wayside, disfigured by ugly wounds. Perhaps their devotion to ritual purity cost them the spontaneity of love found in resonant attuning. If so, their devotion—rigidly adhered to—served as a secondary incentive for good. Possibly being locked in by legislated duties perverted their freedom and blinded them to their Desire that

SECOND NATURE

When our sacred Desire is met with unrepaired or traumatic dissonant attuning, we grow in fear, we act defensively, we view the world as fundamentally bad, and we morally judge life. We grow into unwholeness as the diagram below illustrates.

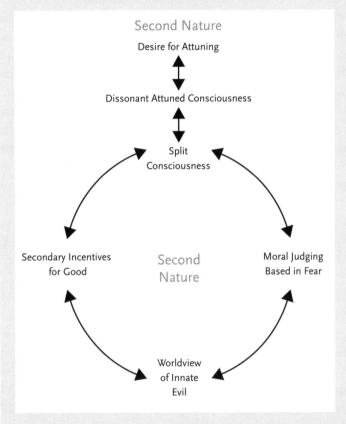

Repair of dissonant attuning experiences requires awareness of them, which causes suffering. This is not to recommend suffering.

would have freed them to see the other as a person to be redeemed by love. It was not the ritual purity or legislated duties per se that distorted their Desire and sidetracked them into their Second Nature. It was their being locked into those duties. It was their being blinded by those duties so that, in this instance, they did not respond to help the half-dead man. Neither of them created a "we-centric" space, a womb of compassion, for him. They saw only that their behavior of attending to their temple duties was the right thing to do. They were blind to what was more important—the needs of the man in the ditch.

We deeply crave connection with the Divine through resonant attuning with each other, which ignites our Desire. We experience fear, despair, and rage when that is denied. With our bodies full of fear, despair, and rage, we carry these distortions out into the world with us. It is still a world perceived through intersubjective sensitivity, but our perceptions derive from dissonant attuning with others. We feel bad, and we experience the world as evil.

When we experience the world as evil—whether or not we explicitly or consciously articulate this worldview—we hold four beliefs as undisputable truth. First, we believe that evil is primary and inevitable—we believe that it exists from the beginning of time. Second, we believe that an injurious force called violence is inherent in our being; we believe that we are born with destructive

---

If suffering alone taught, all of us would be wise. But it encourages us to endure our suffering in order to shift from Second to First Nature. Suffering in our Second Nature, when our sacred Desire is distorted, leaves us bitter. Suffering in our First Nature, when we live in synchrony with our sacred Desire, gives us compassion.

Source: Nancy K. Morrison and Sally K. Severino, "The Biology of Morality," *Zygon: Journal of Religion and Science* 38, no. 4 (2003): 855–69.

impulses. Third, we believe that violence can be managed only by channeling its expression. And fourth, stronger violence seems to eradicate less strong violence, leading to the conclusion that violence fixes things.[3]

Walter Wink, professor of biblical interpretation at Auburn Theological Seminary in New York, recognizes this worldview as the "myth of redemptive violence."[4] He explains that when we believe in the myth of redemptive violence, we split the world into good and evil and declare ourselves to be on one side, ordinarily the side that we define as the "good" side. We deny our capability and culpability for evil, and project all evil onto another person, country, or other readily identifiable group. Seeing the other person or group as evil frees us to direct violence toward them with impunity. The myth states that when we are humiliated or violated, we set things right by striking back and by killing off the evil(doers) that caused our pain. Though blind to it, we become caught up in the comfort and certitude of self-righteousness. We feel powerful and capable of redeeming our injured selves, and perhaps even our injured nation or world.

In this worldview—constructed when we are in our Second Nature—we and our morality are distorted. Instead of valuing others and ourselves, we judge our behavior and the behavior of others and apply rules to others and ourselves with the conviction that we can eliminate evil by force.[5] Kathryn Watterson tells the true story of a man who lived as though all of his capacity for valuing was in the form of judging. He judged "niggers," "Jew boys," and anyone who was not white "Aryan" Christian to be evil and attempted to rid the world of them. The man was Larry Trapp, Grand Dragon of the White Knights of the Ku Klux Klan of Nebraska. Watterson writes:

> [I] sat in the middle of a terrorist's mind and experience and wrote
> about it. . . . Over time, I . . . began to see the terrible isolation
> and self-loathing that direct such a life. It is filled with anguish,

unresolved terrors, grief, rage, depression, isolation and secrecy. Larry Trapp, who was taught the habits of hate when he was a small, abused child, felt confused, humiliated and insignificant. As he grew to be a man, guns quelled some of his fears, and hatred made him feel more powerful. To appear bigger, tougher and meaner, he spoke with his fists, acquired more weapons and built more bombs—externalizing his rage, blaming and diminishing those around him.[6]

Viewed from the outside, Larry Trapp's perspective blinded him to his own perpetuation of cruelty and evil. His actions revealed

BRAKING OUR ATTUNING

If we are so built to attune to one another, how do we stop ourselves from being captured by another's nervous system? Scientists have suggested three brakes that we can use.

- Selection. We select what we see. Were we to attend to all information that comes to our brains at any one time, we would be overloaded. So, our brain censors what we see before we are aware of it.

- Stopping ourselves. After the activation of mirror neurons, we can stop ourselves before we imitate the other's actions. In other words, we can stop the imitative motor action or substitute another action. Instead of yawning when we see another yawn, for example, we can swallow instead.

- Inhibiting ourselves. We can consciously and deliberately dose our degree of resonance with another depending on our trust or mistrust of them.

Sources: Daniel N. Stern, *The Present Moment in Psychotherapy and Everyday Life* (New York: W. W. Norton, 2004), 82; Jeffrey M. Schwartz and Sharon Begley, *The Mind and The Brain: Neuroplasticity and the Power of Mental Force* (New York: HarperCollins, 2002).

that he believed the problem of evil could be solved only by violence, his violence toward others. He operated from self-righteousness and humiliated fury, believing that God—not the God of love and justice, but the God of judgment, vengeance, and retribution—called him to right the wrongs that he perceived were done against him. Convinced that his views were God's views, he believed that his actions—no matter how heinous—were God's actions. In short, he transmogrified himself and his actions into God. This was not union with the Holy, but disunion—a distortion of his Desire for oneness with God—the results of which were ever-spiraling violence, increased hatred, and deepening self-righteousness, self-denial, and ultimately God-denial. The irony of his worldview, of course, was that as he destroyed others, he was also destroying himself and the intimacy and authenticity of his relationship with the Divine.

Frequently, the distortion of Desire gets expressed less dramatically in our lives. A psychiatric resident, Jeremy, whom Sally supervised, provides us one example. His patient, Fred, a fifty-nine-year-old man suffering from depression, described a childhood of repeated incidents of dissonant attuning with his parents.

"When I was ten, I brought home a stray dog and asked my mother's permission to keep it. She ran an ad in the newspaper and when no one claimed the dog, she allowed me to keep Pal. Two years later, when a man claimed that Pal was his, he and Mother decided that since they were both Catholics, they would ask the priest about rightful dog-ownership. The priest decided that I must give Pal to the man. I cried for days. I had lost a good friend." His emotionally distant mother responded to her son's grief by shaming him for crying. [Fred's mother was unable to resonantly attune to his pain.]

Fred's unrepaired experience of shame, together with repeated interactions of unrepaired dissonant attuning—intended to teach him to behave properly—contributed to his identity as an adult of behaving according to what was considered "socially right." [In order for Fred to feel like a "good" son, he endorsed his mother's fear-based value of doing the right thing.]

His identity as a person who always did the right thing led to four failed marriages where Fred unhesitatingly married a woman, not out of strong physical and emotional attraction but to satisfy "should" and because "it was the thing to do." He described these relationships as a consequence of "rational decision making" and said "emotions don't enter into it." In his relationships with women he tried to avoid the pain of shame by keeping his thoughts and emotions separate from each other. These relationships left him unsatisfied and yearning for true connection.

His relationships with men were also troubled. Although Fred denied his need for connection, he was desperately hungry for connection to someone. During his psychotherapy with Jeremy, he met a man who paid an inordinate amount of attention to him. He felt so elated that in his excitement he agreed to play a role where the other man swindled someone out of money. Fred's hunger for relationship was so intense that he mistakenly believed he was experiencing resonant attuning when, instead, he was being manipulated. He impulsively connected at any cost. This behavior, intended to disavow his shameful self who always did what he "should," actually produced a situation that rendered him ashamed.

Fred's Desire had become distorted by shame. Each of us has experienced times when our Desire for loving recognition has been met with dissonant attuning that has gone unrepaired. This leaves us feeling we have no pleasurable value to the loved other. Moreover, unrepaired dissonant attuning leaves us despising our self and ashamed of our Desire. We bury these painful feelings and keep our need for love locked away because we fear being met with dissonant attuning and shame. But our unmet need continues to grow, as Fred's did.

This can lead us to fear our own goodness. Fear *of* goodness results from a vicious negative cycle. We are met by dissonant attuning that remains unrepaired. This leaves us despising our self and ashamed of our Desire. We bury our Desire that is now linked with our despised self. Our unmet need for love grows. At the same time, our shame-distorted Desire and our despised self become so

MEMORY'S ROLE IN REPAIRING DISSONANT ATTUNING

At birth the human brain contains an estimated one hundred billion brain cells. Each cell, called a neuron, makes from zero to two hundred thousand connections to other neurons. And each connection made by two neurons is an elementary unit of memory.

Twentieth-century scientific studies of memory have disclosed three different kinds of memory.

- Working memory is where we hold information long enough to complete a task. It is transient.

- Short-term memory, which is more stable than working memory, does not require protein synthesis and does not produce structural change in the brain.

- Long-term memory requires protein synthesis that leads to changes in neuron connectivity and to alterations in patterns of neuron firing in the brain.

We propose that when we repair dissonant attuning experiences, we change our long-term memory so that neuron connections that were made in dissonant attuning are now remade in resonant attuning. This can lead the brain to grow into neural integration, which enables flexibility and self-understanding as well as increased capacity for rewarding interpersonal relationships.

Sources: David J. Linden, *The Accidental Mind* (Cambridge: The Belknap Press of Harvard University Press, 2007); Erik R. Kandel, "Biology and the Future of Psychoanalysis: A New Intellectual Framework for Psychiatry Revisited," *American Journal of Psychiatry* 156, no. 4 (1999): 505–24; Daniel J. Siegel, *The Mindful Brain: Reflection and Attunement in the Cultivation of Well-being* (New York: W. W. Norton, 2007); Larry R. Squire and Eric R. Kandel, *Memory: From Mind to Molecules* (New York: Scientific American Library, 1999).

intertwined that we can't experience our Desire without simultaneously experiencing shame and rage. Because we do not want our despised and enraged self to be seen, we fear our goodness. Ultimately, however, our distorted Desire will get expressed and we will need to deal with the consequences.

Fred's Desire was so distorted and his Holy Spark so covered over by his "doing what he should" that he made a wrong moral decision. But he didn't stop there. He went on to show us a paradox. He showed us a potential benefit of a secondary incentive for good. It can create a relationship—such as Fred's relationship with Jeremy—that will allow us to accept responsibility for a wrong moral decision.

For Fred, the production of a shame experience during his psychotherapy invited Jeremy to name his participation in the swindle without condemnation or shaming. This created a new experience for the patient. Experiencing Jeremy's respectful resonant attuning, balanced with Jeremy's respectful acceptance of societal needs, fostered a new way of being in relationship for Fred. In his relationship with Jeremy he could experience himself as acceptable and good despite feeling ashamed.

> "How could I have been so unseeing of the serious consequences
> of my behavior?" he asked himself. "I had ample time to con-
> sider beforehand whether or not to participate in the swindle." As
> he explored this observation with Jeremy, he became aware of how
> shame, which he denied, diminished or changed all of his observing
> capacities. As his capacity for managing shame experiences grew, his
> behaviors aimed at avoiding shame diminished.

Jeremy and Fred teach us an important lesson: By delineating the details of our secondary incentives for good, our Desire is "reexposed to shame/guilt so that the individual can reevaluate his or her behavior and can accept himself or herself more completely, love himself or herself more fully, and, secondarily, then can enlarge his or her capacity for a primary incentive for good."[7]

PSYCHOTHERAPY AND RE-MEMBERING

Psychologist Francine Shapiro builds her entire treatment of trauma victims on the premise that an event in a victim's life is stored in memory in a way that is not adaptive because it is not integrated with other memories. The information from such an event (the images, thoughts, sounds, emotions and physical sensations, beliefs) is sequestered and not processed. This allows them to be reexperienced at another time in life unchanged.

Shapiro's treatment, described in her book *Eye Movement Desensitization and Reprocessing,* accesses a specific memory. If, for example, the specific memory is of helplessness, she then identifies a current maladaptive belief related to it such as *I am helpless.* This memory evokes the person's emotional and bodily experiences of the maladaptive belief, which she uses to measure the progress of reprocessing the old memory. For example, the person who believes *I am helpless* might recall a specific memory from childhood. The memory of the adult evokes the same emotions of fear and helplessness that she experienced in her gut and heart as a child. The adult is asked to rate the intensity of her gut and heart disturbance on a scale of 0 to 10.

Following this she would choose a preferred belief such as *I can take care of myself.* Selection of a preferred belief begins the location of another neural network to which the negative belief can be

Fred—in his relating to Jeremy—gives us a glimpse of how we human beings can use our wounds as a key to our moving through and beyond distortion. In the next chapter, we will explore in more depth how we can reconfigure our past and ourselves to bring us from our Second Nature back into our First Nature.

linked. A process of neural reintegration ensues where the preferred belief is connected with the old memory network. Reintegration occurs from repeated practice of holding together the old memory with the preferred belief. This strengthens the preferred belief and weakens the maladaptive belief reflected in less intense gut and heart disturbance.

As Shapiro's treatment indicates, neural networks do not change with learning in adulthood in the same way that they were laid down in our brains by way of experience when we were growing up. For new learning to occur, novel experience must become linked with memories. This requires our paying attention. So we must pay attention to both the past (the memory) and to the present (the novel event). The novel event in the example above is the preferred belief and the emotional and bodily experiences associated with it. Memories and beliefs of greatest emotional value will excite and/or inhibit our efforts to pay attention to new events. Even when we sense a new experience, beliefs will excite and/or inhibit our efforts to link it with the stored memory expectation that we want to change. In other words, we cannot just erase old memories. Instead, we modify them and the structure of the brain that stores them by adding a new memory, which, in the example of the person who believed she was helpless, was the experience of feeling that she could take care of herself.

In the work of Francine Shapiro, her relationship with her trauma victim becomes a new memory. Within this relationship of resonant attuning, Shapiro enhances learning the new experience by using sensory stimulation like eye movement or hand tapping. To decrease the strength of the old memory, for example, she will ask the person to follow her finger visually while recalling the memory and the negative belief. She will do the same to increase the strength of the new memory, both the positive belief and the experience of the resonantly attuning relationship.

Sidebar continues

Psychotherapy and Re-membering, *continued*

How sensory stimulation works remains unknown, but several hypotheses exist. One is that sensory stimulation interferes with working memory by disrupting visual and spatial functions. Another is that it elicits an orienting response where interest and excitement in a preferred belief can be linked to maladaptive stored information. Alternatively, perhaps sensory stimulation evokes a relaxation response where new physiological states and responses can be linked with the maladaptive stored information. Or, perhaps it activates a neurological process similar to the kind of information processing that occurs nightly during rapid eye movement sleep (dream sleep).

Other mental health professionals enhance the learning of new information with different techniques such as insight-oriented psychotherapy. Regardless of technique, memory builds identity from our past, maintains identity in the present, and becomes the means for changing our identity in the future.

Source: Francine Shapiro, *Eye Movement Desensitization and Reprocessing: Basic Principles, Protocols, and Procedures,* 2nd ed. (New York: Guilford Press, 2001).

CHAPTER 6

BEYOND DISTORTION

Reconfiguring Our Past Today

> Look deeply and you will touch the fact that happi-
> ness and well-being cannot be separated from suf-
> fering and ill-being. This is the interbeing nature of
> happiness and suffering.
>
> —THICH NHAT HANH

O UR SACRED DESIRE draws us toward those who see us as we truly are and reflect back that we are loved. When this happens, our experiences affirm—through resonant attuning—our First Nature. We feel "happiness and well-being," according to Thich Nhat Hanh.[1]

Thich Nhat Hanh also recognizes that happiness and suffering cannot be separated. We are both our First Nature, which grew from those experiences where we were met with resonant attuning that brought us happiness, and our Second Nature, which grew from those experiences where we were met with dissonant attuning that brought us suffering. As we proceed through life, the energy of Desire urges us to transform our Second Nature into our First Nature. It urges us to move beyond distortion by reconfiguring our past. The experience of Larry, who came to Nancy for help, illustrates this:

Larry's early childhood was generally a happy one until a teenage cousin and his friend sexually molested him. Afraid to tell his parents, Larry carefully kept the molestation secret. Yet he longed for his parents to notice his pain. Though he felt broken and unlovable, Larry intuitively knew that if his parents could acknowledge his brokenness, their comfort and consolation would assure him that he was loved, that wholeness was possible, and that he could be helped to find that wholeness.

Unfortunately, because Larry was too ashamed to reveal his molestation, his parents remained oblivious to his distress.

As he grew up, Larry was an obedient son, a model student, and an excellent musician, but inside he felt defective, frightened, and incompetent. He feared that if people knew the truth about him, they would reject him, as it seemed to him that his parents had. Finally, in his mid-twenties, Larry's anguish drove him to therapy with Nancy. Larry's relief was obvious when Nancy accepted the pain he experienced. Over the ensuing weeks he was able to work on sources of that pain to bring further relief.

But Nancy sensed that there was something more. She asked, "You've held that awful pain inside for a long time, Larry. How did you manage to deal with it?" Long moments passed. Finally Larry said quietly, "When I was fourteen, I went to church camp. As usual, I felt I didn't belong. Everyone else seemed so happy and carefree, which made me feel even more lonely and depressed. One afternoon, I went for a walk." He hesitated, then continued: "Eventually I found a quiet place under a tree by a stream. I sat down on a big rock, listened to the water, and prayed." Looking away, he went on: "I felt this warm, loving presence. It was Jesus, and he assured me that, no matter what I felt, I was deeply loved," Larry's voice broke, "and lovable."

Nancy replied gently, "Clearly that was a profound spiritual experience for you." Larry looked at her and said, "I thought if I told you this story, you'd think I was really crazy." She smiled and said, "No. You're not crazy. Jesus was there with you in your pain. What was that like for you?" Larry then shared how this experience, and his memory of it, sustained him over the years.

When Nancy accepted Larry's encounter with Jesus as one of great importance and respected it as a true spiritual experience, he developed a new level of trust in their relationship. As his trust grew, his sense of disconnection decreased. Gradually he began to let go of his shame and his perception of himself as defective, frightened, and incompetent. The connection that he'd experienced with Jesus now moved him to a deeper level in his relationship with Nancy, which opened the door to further insights. Those insights allowed him to view himself in a new and holy light, and to live his life—with himself, others, and God—with an integrity, an openness, and a joy that he'd never experienced before.

Reflecting on Larry's experience, we see that his Desire was for his parents to see him as he truly was—the molested child—and to let him know that he was loved. Because he did not find this, the trauma of molestation distorted his Desire. Indeed, it distorted his whole being—spiritual, biological, and psychological. All aspects of his personhood would need reconfiguration in order for him to modify his Second Nature and be able to live more of the time in his First Nature.

The foundation for moving beyond his distortion came at birth. Larry's parents had, at the very least, given him as an infant and young child, sufficient affection and stimulation to enable him to survive his childhood trauma. He survived, but his distorted Desire manifested itself in his feeling broken and unlovable.

To some degree, Larry moved beyond these feelings when he encountered Jesus. This encounter revitalized his Desire for connection with the spiritual and reaffirmed that he was loved and lovable. This experience motivated him (albeit unconsciously) to seek further restoration and to ask for Nancy's help. Larry's therapy illustrates how a relationship can move us toward wholeness. We believe that resonant attuning relationships—such as therapy —utilize our mirror neurons to change our brains and us.

Nancy's capacity to be with Larry in his pain—developed as her unique expression of the Divine, honed through her psychiatric training, and informed by her own spiritual seeking—enabled new neural pathways to be forged in his brain. Through

CONTINUUM OF INDIVIDUAL FUNCTIONING

The brain develops functions and capacities that reflect repetitive experiences. In childhood, resonant attuning experiences build love-based responses into the developing brain. Dissonant attuning experiences build in fear-based responses. These responses can be seen in emotional, cognitive, and behavioral functioning.

Attuning Arousal	Subjective State	Regulating Brain Region	Cognitive Style	Sense of Time	Dissociation Continuum	Arousal Continuum
Resonant	Calm	Neocortex	Abstract	Extended Future	Rest	Rest
Nontraumatic Dissonant	Aroused	Cortex	Concrete	Days	Avoidance	Vigilance
	Alarmed	Limbic	Emotional	Hours	Compliance	Resistance
Traumatic Dissonant	Fear	Midbrain	Reactive	Minutes	Dissociation	Defiance
	Terror	Brain stem (automatic)	Reflexive	Lost	Fainting (freeze)	Aggression

When trauma occurs, two primary response patterns occur that often alternate within us. They are shown in the two right-hand columns: dissociative continuum responses (defeat responses such as distraction, numbing, and fainting) and arousal continuum responses (fight or flight responses). If the neurobiology of dissociation and arousal responses are activated long enough, there will be molecular, structural, and functional changes in the brain. In other words, a state will become a trait that habitually determines how information from the world is retrieved and processed.

Source: Adapted from: Bruce D. Perry, "The Neurodevelopmental Impact of Violence in Childhood," in *Textbook of Child and Adolescent Forensic Psychiatry,* ed. D. Schetky and E. Benedek (Washington, D.C.: American Psychiatric Press, 2001), 221–38.

resonant attuning she offered a safe place where he could reveal his experiences and realize his Desire, which was to be one with the Divine and to animate his own holiness. The spiral of restoration to wholeness then continued as Larry learned to love himself and others in a new and more gratifying way.

Reconfiguring our past begins with the felt experience of being loved as Larry experienced with Jesus. Physiologically, this moved Larry from the traumatic experience of molestation into resonant attuning with Jesus—a ventral vagal parasympathetic state. This new physiology later allowed him the relative comfort to enter into a relational exchange with Nancy. Emotionally, he moved increasingly from a state of suffering and ill-being to a state of feeling comforted, understood, and being cared for. Biologically, he moved from a state of fear to a state of love. Psychologically, he moved from anxiety to calm, and spiritually, he moved from mistrust to trust. His relationship with Nancy (more than being "in therapy") solidified his love of God and self; it also opened him to the possibility of loving others. Socioculturally, he used his Christian teaching/teachers of love to sustain him while he lived with parents who were not resonantly attuning to him and with relatives who abused him. Ultimately, love allowed him to seek psychiatric care.

We conclude that the determining factors for Larry's—and our—moving beyond distortion are "(a) the extent to which the person is capable of loving himself or herself deeply, and (b) the capacity the person has for trusting and valuing the other."[2] The ability to experience love of self requires being received in resonant attuning by another. A trustworthy person who can genuinely value us must provide this resonant attuning.

Paradoxically, these factors can also move us into harmful relationships. We are created for relationship and love. When two people in their Second Nature attune to each other, it may feel like resonant attuning. But such attuning expresses both a distortion of our Desire as well as our attempt to get back into our First Nature. We saw an example of this when Jeremy's patient, Fred, got pulled into a swindle by a con man.

Reconfiguring our past requires recognizing that we are whole people who live in both our First and Second Nature, and recognizing that our biological, psychological, and spiritual aspects are intimately—and wondrously—connected. Because we are truly whole people, then psychological or physical abuse is also spiritual abuse, and spiritual abuse also violates our psychological and

MEMORY'S ROLE IN RECONFIGURING OUR PAST TODAY

Early in life, all memories are stored as implicit memories of behavioral, emotional, perceptual, and bodily experiences that are known without being thought. Christopher Bollas calls them the "unthought known." Most of us do not consciously recall these memories from our early years, but undeniably we repeat these states physiologically and we re-experience these feeling states emotionally. Early attachment patterns are implicit memories.

Likewise, procedural information—like riding a bicycle—is stored as implicit memories. Riding a bicycle, once learned, is performed without any forethought. Motions are the automatic product of previously stored performance information.

The explicit memory system requires the hippocampus, which needs years of neurodevelopment to become functional. This system encodes event memories, including autobiographical recollections and discrete facts.

Who we are and who we become depends, in part, on our memories.

physical well-being. They are interrelated and affect our functioning. If one aspect is hurt, they all hurt. If one person hurts, we all hurt. This is the extended meaning of Thich Nhat Hanh's concept of "interbeing"—we are called to wholeness, to live in love, embracing our interbeing nature of happiness and suffering, and embracing our interbeing with the being of all.

In our next chapter, we will begin addressing explicit steps in the healing power of Desire. Before we do that, two general observations are helpful. First, unrepaired trauma is ongoing and is

Memory Processes		
Process	Brain Region	Action
Encoding	Hippocampus	Makes what we sense and think into a brain record
Storage	Brain circuits that do not involve the hippocampus	Implicit memory (procedural information)
		No sense of self, time, or remembering
		Is available at birth
	Hippocampus involved	Explicit memory (declarative information)
		Acquires facts—memories for people, objects, places Requires focused attention
Consolidation	Cortex	Makes a short-term memory into a long-term memory
Retrieval	Before consolidation, requires the hippocampus	Retrieval of autobiographical narrative

Sources: Christopher Bollas, The Shadow of the Object: Psychoanalysis of the Unthought Known (New York: Columbia University Press, 1987); Larry R. Squire and Eric R. Kandel, Memory: From Mind to Molecules (New York: Scientific American Library, 1999).

more difficult to reconfigure. Second, what looks like trauma isn't necessarily so.

Unrepaired trauma. Let us return to Larry, whose story shows us how trauma that is unrepaired is ongoing and difficult to reconfigure. His continuing experiences of shame kept triggering in Larry the physiological state that kept the trauma alive. With each re-experience, the unrepaired neural networks in his brain became more automatic and habitual, more resistant to change. They also competed with networks created in resonant attuning.

While Larry's healing began at age fourteen when Jesus appeared to him, his trauma wasn't more fully repaired until a decade later. Further repair continued when he could disclose his molestation and ongoing distress to Nancy within a resonant attuning relationship over time. Not everyone needs a psycho-therapeutic relationship. The need for psychotherapy depends on the nature and severity of injury caused by the trauma and on the wholeness of the people with whom the injured person interacts. What is important is the interacting—in resonant attuning—with people who are as whole as possible. The living experience of reso-nant attuning heals us and reconfigures our distorted Desire.

During the healing process, the injured person may pull the other person—through their mutual attuning—into his or her dis-tortedness. This does not necessarily mean that the other person is permanently damaged. It simply means that we are influenced by each other. That influence seems mandatory. It gives the injured person the opportunity to see how he personally disappoints the other. That vis-à-vis can keep us watchful of when we are out of sync with our Desire and with the Desire of another.

Not really trauma. Depending on how it is perceived, what looks like trauma on first glance can be a part of life that leads to happi-ness and well-being, as Thich Nhat Hahn discerned. An outstand-ing example is our friend, Minda Cox, who lives this truth daily. In 1988 she was born without arms and legs to a young married couple in India who were unable to care for such a baby. Other young couples, especially fathers, in that country in that year might have let the newborn girl die. Instead, her father took one-day-old Minda to a hospital in Manipal many miles away, hoping that someone could care for her. Not only did he keep her alive, he claimed her by leaving his name as well as the name of her mother. The hospital called her Prashna, meaning "question," because no one knew what would become of her.

She stayed at the hospital until she was seven months old when she was placed in the Ashraya Children's Home in Bangalore. There she was given the name Swapma, meaning "dream." Her unique disability required people to touch and care for her. She could do nothing for herself. This touching stimulated Minda's capacity for resonant attuning and nourished her sacred Desire.

By coincidence, the Ashraya Children's Home was the home from which Cathy Cox, an American single mother, had previously adopted one of her four older children, three of whom had special needs. Cathy read about Minda in the home's newsletter. When she read that this child would never be adopted because caring for a child who would always lie on her back would be so difficult, Cathy thought, "The child needs to be around other disabled kids."

Cathy flew to India from the United States. When first setting eyes on Minda, Cathy saw something special in her. She told us, "I thought this is a baby with courage and this is a baby with love for life. She was a happy child, wasn't afraid and wasn't shy, so I thought she'll be fine."

It took fifteen months for Cathy to bring twenty-two-month-old Minda to the United States because the toddler could not provide a thumbprint for a passport. India's Supreme Court had to approve a passport without one.

Minda Catherine Deenaz (her Indian social worker's name) Cox is the one child named after Cathy, who wanted Minda to know she was proud of her most visibly disabled child.

Over the years Cathy continued to foster Minda's growth into First Nature. One of the fruits of their mutual resonant attuning has been Minda's becoming mobile. Not only did she not lie on her back all her life, she learned to scoot around on the floor and to use an electric wheelchair.

Another fruit has been Minda's becoming an accomplished watercolor artist who paints by holding the brush between her chin and her shoulder. After her first art exhibit, eighteen-year-old Minda told us, "The Lord has created me with a physical disability that I can never run away from. God has shown me His love and goodness in everything He's done for me because of, and in the middle of, my inability to be totally independent. Therefore my purpose in life is to show others my joy that God is good all the time, and that nothing in life is outside God's love and ability to turn it to good."

Imagination also played a role in Minda's life. Imagination is somehow tied to the capacity to create or forge new and different neural pathways that lead us to personal and spiritual growth. It allowed Minda to see how she could paint although she had no arms. Not only did she learn to paint, she earned enough money through selling her art to pay for her, Cathy, her art teacher, and her art teacher's husband to go to India in January 2008 for the twenty-fifth anniversary of the Ashraya Children's Home.

While there, local newspapers and CNN-IBN photographers and reporters captured Minda's story and broadcast her desire to meet her Indian family. They quoted her as saying, "I want to thank them for keeping me alive, and I want to show them that I am fine." Minda's father's brother, who lives in Bangalore, read the newspaper story. He called Ashraya and also Minda's seventeen-year-old sister, Pavithra, who was working at a garment factory in Bangalore. The two of them met Minda and helped with arrangements for Minda to meet her first parents, Kalavathi and Shankar Shetty, in their house in Kolekebailu in the Udupi District.

When Minda, Cathy, Minda's art teacher and husband, plus a translator drove down the narrow, rutted footpath to the Shettys' small house, they couldn't see the house at all. Over two hundred villagers crowded around it waiting for "our baby" to show up. Her parents had to make their way through the crowd to get to the car.

When Kalavathi, Minda's first mother, looked into the open door of the car, Minda leaned right into her and—wrapping the little stumps of her arms around her neck—pulled her into the car where Kalavathi immediately embraced Minda and wept, as did Minda. When Shankar finally got the wheelchair out, he proudly pushed his daughter into the house. Inside, Minda met her two other sisters, fifteen-year-old Pallavi and thirteen-year-old Chaitra, her very elderly grandparents, and many relatives. "Wow," she exclaimed. "I'm not in a sea of blondes for once." In the United States Minda is the youngest of five. In India she is "akka," the honored oldest sister.

Minda even received a visit from Dr. Mohan, who was one of the doctors that cared for her when Shankar left her at the hospital. He brought her pictures that had been taken of her as a baby.

Minda's family gave her small and precious gifts and Minda gave Kalavathi spectacularly beautiful purple material for a sari that she had purchased the previous day. She also gave material for a shirt to Shankar and material to her sisters. They all shared food and Minda's family delighted in seeing her enjoy the new tastes. They spent two days together.

Throughout the visit Minda had eyes above all for Kalavathi who told her, "It is good he [Shankar] took you when you were one day old. If he had waited until you were two days old, I would not have let you go." And Minda knew it was true. Minda recalls that the first words Kalavathi spoke to Cathy were "I may have given birth to her, but you have given her life." Minda delighted in seeing her two mothers accepting each other.

It was obvious that Shankar had worked hard to move his family from the mud hut into which Minda was born to a small cement house with a tiled roof, two cows, and a few chickens. A cheerful, charming, guileless man, he had educated his three daughters, who are all dear girls. Pallavi and Minda made promises to write each other. But Kalavathi was the one whom Minda longed to see, and she filled her eyes with Kalavathi's face, as did Kalavathi gazing at Minda.

The next day Kalavathi looked like a queen in her new sari and Shankar looked like a king in his new shirt. Amazingly, both sari and shirt had been sewn overnight from the material Minda had given them!

After a day of laughing, talking, and trying to put nineteen years of story into a few hours, Kalavathi gave Minda a lovely green shirt and fitted a tiny silver bracelet on Minda's little stump of a leg because Minda had admired her sister's.

Minda now says she feels "complete." For all nineteen years of her life she had wanted to be reassured by her birth parents that they loved her, that they were not ashamed of her, and that they had not kept her secret. Kalavathi and Shankar left Minda with no doubts on any score. And Minda left them with no doubts about what they had done in keeping her alive. Unanswered questions from all their pasts were answered within their mutual resonant attuning, allowing the First Nature of each person to be reconfigured through their love of each other. Minda says it all, "It's so good now to be my own story."

In the next chapter we will present explicit steps that we can all use to access the healing power of sacred Desire.

CHAPTER 7

THE HEALING POWER OF DESIRE

Practical Steps to Loving Self and Others

> For Mercy has a human heart
> Pity, a human face:
> And Love, the human form divine,
> And Peace, the human dress.
>
> —WILLIAM BLAKE, "THE DIVINE IMAGE"

THE HEALING POWER of Desire brings us into what Blake names, "Love, the human form divine."[1] When our Desire meets and fits resonantly with the Desire of another who is in his or her First Nature, both of us are in harmony with the Divine, and we are free to let ourselves be given in love to each other. The call of love, the call of *agape*, is the goal of our being. Our purpose is to constitute each other by loving each other.

The best analogy for understanding how we constitute each other is the hologram. We are each like a hologram with our individual sacred Desire that has been given us in our genes. Individually we are complete creations. But individually we are not a whole creation. For creation to be whole, each of us must meet and fit in harmony with others who are in First Nature.

Bodily we are created to love our self and others. So much of our human brain—almost the whole right hemisphere—is made to take us into relationship. We stay healthy by staying in relationship, by turning to another person in love and inviting that person into the mutuality of love. Just as parents ignite their child's Desire, our continuing spiritual maturation involves relationships that change our brain, allowing us to love more fully and not be stressed out by troublesome people who are those living in their Second Nature.

This entails surrendering to the healing power of our sacred Desire. As Professor of Humanities Rita Brock states:

> We are broken by the world of our relationships before we are able to defend ourselves. It is not a damage we willfully choose. Those who damage us do not have the power to heal us, for they themselves are

THE PROCESS OF RE-MEMBERING

Long-term memory is vital for repairing experiences of dissonant attuning, a process that involves remembering those experiences and then making new brain connections. In other words, we re-member—literally re-make—our neural networks. We revisit parts of our self in order to allow memories that have been stored as dissonant attuning experiences to be re-experienced within resonant attuning to form new neural connections. This restructures our brain into more integrated patterns.

The process of re-membering dissonant attuning experiences:

1. First, begins with retrieving memories. To do this we must want to retrieve memories; and when those memories are not in our awareness, we need strong motivation.

2. Second, continues with realizing that our environment influences what we remember. Our environment shapes what we recall and influences our subjective experience of remembering.

not healed. To be healed, we must take responsibility for recognizing our own damage by following our hearts to the relationships that will empower our self-healing. In living by heart, we are called not to absolve ourselves of the consequences of an inherited flaw. We are called to remember our own brokenheartedness, the extent of our vulnerability, and the depth of our need for relationships. Hence we are called not to dependence on power outside ourselves, but to an exploration of the depths of our most inner, personal selves as the root of our connections to all others.[2]

In essence, coming into "Love, the human form divine" involves reestablishing the womb of compassion.[3] We offer seven steps through which Desire can heal us and move us from brokenheartedness to the womb of compassion—to love of self and others. It is a process that can begin at any point in life, at any age.

This fact is important because whom we select to help us heal will influence our subjective experience of remembering.

3. Third, requires selecting another to help us. We need a trusted other or others to modify our memories. Memories made in relationships of unrepaired dissonant attuning distort our Desire. Changing those memories so that they do not distort our Desire requires reliving them in a relationship of resonant attuning.

As psychologist Diana Fosha explains in her book *The Transforming Power of Affect*, "There is . . . such a thing as the in-the-moment *experience* of one's true or essential self, and it is . . . [an] experience of authenticity . . . " Living in-the-moment authentically in resonant attuning happens when all aspects of our being mutually interact and when that authentic essence expresses our sacred Desire.

Source: Diana Fosha, *The Transforming Power of Affect: A Model for Accelerated Change* (New York: Basic Books, 2000), 32.

Step 1: Awakening: becoming aware of how our distorted Desire results in distorted ways of connecting with others physically, psychologically, and spiritually.

Very simply this means waking up. We wake up to each secondary incentive for good and how it is sidetracking us from trusting into mistrusting Desire. A local New York newspaper carried the following Associated Press story. We have changed all names, including the name of the store. This story shows us the secondary incentive for good of wanting to possess things rather than valuing relationships.

A mob of shoppers rushing for a sale on DVD players trampled the first woman in line and knocked her unconscious as they scrambled for the shelves at a shopping center.

Lois Lancaster had her eye on a $29 DVD player, but when the siren blared at 6 a.m. Friday announcing the start to the post-Thanksgiving sale, the 41-year-old was knocked to the ground by the frenzy of shoppers behind her.

"She got pushed down, and they walked over her like a herd of elephants," said Lancaster's sister, Ilene. "I told them, 'Stop stepping on my sister! She's on the ground!'"

Ilene said some shoppers tried to help Lois, and one employee helped Ilene reach her sister, but most people just continued their rush for deals.

"All they cared about was a stupid DVD player," she said yesterday.

Paramedics called to the store found Lois unconscious on top of a DVD player, surrounded by shoppers seemingly oblivious to her, said Matt Brooks, a spokesman for the emergency ambulance.

She was flown to North Medical, where doctors told the family she had a seizure after she was knocked down and would likely remain hospitalized through the weekend, Ilene said. Hospital officials said yesterday they did not have any information on her condition.

Ilene said the shopping center officials called later Friday to ask about her sister, and the store offered to put a DVD player on hold for her.

The store's spokeswoman Marilyn Brockbent said she had never heard of such a melee during a sale.

"We are very disappointed this happened," Brockbent said. "We want her to come back as a shopper."

Newspapers are full of stories like this. We have structured our world such that buying is sacred and shopping is both retail therapy and holy. Competing for the best and the most has become the measure of our being. In this story competition sidetracked shoppers—as it sidetracks us—from their Desire for oneness with each other into forgetting that the other shoppers were part of them.

Fortunately the store's officials took the time to inquire about Lois, but, unfortunately, their Desire—like that of the shoppers—was seemingly distorted by greed. Putting a DVD on hold for her to purchase demonstrated how they continued to value money more than a relationship.

Implicit in the store officials' response is a mistrust of Desire. Had they trusted their Desire, they would have felt remorseful about the melee and wished forgiveness for the part that their store had played in occasioning the event. This stance would not be one of blaming themselves. It would be one of giving up grievances about the melee and feeling sadness that someone had been hurt. It would be a stance of realizing interconnectedness—that they, together with the shoppers, were responsible for what happened. To experience honestly the full range of their emotions—sorrow and responsibility together with desiring restoration of a relationship—could have led to healing.

How does the honesty of seeing clearly and the completeness of experiencing emotions heal us? Perhaps it heals because our earliest memories, our earliest brain networks, are honest, undefended emotional memories. So re-experiencing our honest emotions gets us closest to our earliest sense of integrity. Experiencing emotions without in any way denying or defending against them gives us as adults a sense of mastery in being true to our human nature.

Instead, store spokeswoman Marilyn Brockbent's behavior seemed to express secondary incentives for good. Her comment that she "had never heard of such a melee during a sale" acted to justify the store. And the offer to put a DVD player on hold for Lois served as an appeasement. Both endeavors attempted to shift responsibility away from the store, as though the spokeswoman feared it would be judged morally inadequate either by Lois or by the public. Unfortunately, our world's litigiousness makes it very difficult for the store to take some responsibility for the melee.

This is not to say that Marilyn Brockbent willfully shifted responsibility away from the store. A willful act involves choice and awareness of what she was doing. Shifting responsibility, however, can happen without our knowing it. When we act without awareness, it prevents us from knowing fully what is happening. It also causes us and others harm by keeping parts of ourselves out of relationship and by preventing those excluded aspects of ourselves from growing and changing into more healthy coping strategies.

To become fully aware of what she was doing, Marilyn would have had to experience the pain of the melee. To take responsibility for what happened, she would have had to acknowledge what circumstances determined the melee. Then she would have had to express her intent to find a means for avoiding such events in the future. Taking responsibility would have reflected a compassionate understanding of Lois's experience. It would have expressed a primary incentive for good based in love.

Awareness involves our memory and requires our focused waiting, waiting to know what is wrong, waiting to know how we have contributed to it. Actively looking inward, we wait while the known memory somewhere in us struggles to come into awareness. There are many ways of actively looking inward, including psychotherapy, spiritual practices of prayer and meditation, and our relationships in daily living. All are routes along which Desire can awaken us to the secondary incentive for good that reflects our distorted way of connecting with others.

Awakening invites us to see how our secondary incentive for good once had survival value because it organized our understanding, diminished our pain, and kept us in relationship. Awakening also invites us to see how the secondary incentive for good now limits us by keeping our Desire distorted.

Once we can awaken to our secondary incentive for good, we can dare to share it with another. Because the source of our Desire is relationship within resonant attuning, we enter into such a relationship to change our being. We ask another person to attune to us as we reveal both aspects of our self—our Desire and our defense against it.

Step 2: Naming: articulating our distorted ways of connecting—our secondary incentives for good—within a mutually interactive relationship of trust.

Naming our secondary incentives for good to another is essential for completely understanding how it disrupts relationships. But how do we know whom we can trust?

We can trust people who live predominantly in their First Nature, those who are motivated by a primary incentive for good. Such people have the ability to be present to us in all the complexities of our situation. People who respond in a judgmental way—trying to find someone at fault, determining that someone is bad, advocating predetermined rules of conduct—are probably thinking from secondary incentives for good. Likewise, people committed to institutional imperatives may not be able to be present to our needs. This is not to say that rules are not important; it is to underscore that they are necessary but not sufficient. We need a person who can resonantly attune to us.

Finally, in choosing whom to trust it is important to know how to trust ourself. This is not easy, but the more we know and can trust ourself, the less our own response to another person will lead us astray. The more we know and trust ourself, the more we can trust our sense of whether the other is resonantly attuning to us. We can then safely name our secondary incentives for good.

The following story shows us one example of how naming our secondary incentives for good within a relationship of trust might evolve. Paula had a friend who brought to her attention that she was never home. This invited Paula to look at what her behavior meant.

> Paula's friend once told her, "Whenever I phone you, you are never home. I always have to leave a message on your answering machine." [Her friend names a behavior—Paula's absence—that disrupts their relationship.] The tone of her voice conveys that she cares for Paula. [Her friend's resonant tone of voice allows Paula to tolerate the awareness of her secondary incentive for good.] Paula questions herself, "Why am I never home?" She then realizes that she has organized her life to be away from home at her workplace. This pleases her boss who rewards her efforts with his praise. Being a workaholic also pleases Paula. She has created a place where she feels safe and where she receives praise for her achievements. [Paula's workaholism—her secondary incentive for good—allows her to think of herself as a good person doing good things such as pleasing her boss.]
>
> Realizing that she is absenting herself from home stirs memories of how, as a child, home was never a safe place. [Paula reconnects with her past where the secondary incentive arose.] She confesses to her friend, "I don't like being home. It's a fear that dates to when I was very little. To protect myself from my parents' fury as they fought, I would squeeze my body flat against the floor and slide under our dark vinyl couch. It was my place of sanctuary. But I always knew that they would eventually come after me. For years I endured physical, emotional, and sexual abuse in my outwardly appearing good, Christian family."

Paula's absence from home and her workaholism arose from a fear that was based in memories of early childhood abuse. To cope with her fear she developed secondary incentives for good, her striving for safety and her striving for acknowledgment. When she shared with her friend her fear of being home, it clarified

FEATURES OF SACRED MEMORY

Sacred memory is memory that has been stored in long-term memory within resonant attuning experiences. It:

1. defines our identity.
2. sustains us in community.
3. shapes our hopes for the future.
4. manifests our sacred Desire.

Source: Miroslav Volf, *The End of Memory: Remembering Rightly in a Violent World* (Grand Rapids: Eerdmans, 2006).

how her previously adaptive behavior now limited her current relationship.

Life circumstances very much determine who becomes our resonantly attuning other. In this instance, her telephone friend reached out to Paula. We need such another to listen to us with compassion and without condemnation or rejection in order willingly to open ourselves. Only complete honesty allows us consciously to articulate our hidden fear-filled aspects as well as our good aspects. Only compassion allows us to make our unwelcome aspects into a valued part of our holiness of being. Sharing her secret with her friend allowed Paula to embrace her Desire. It also allowed Paula to permit Desire to bring her into a more realistic and authentic state.

Why do we need to go through this process? Perhaps when we block something from our awareness, we automatically interrupt the spontaneity of attuning. Perhaps by willfully controlling what we dislike about ourselves, we prevent ourselves from satisfying our innate Desire for resonant attuning in relationship.

Perhaps those aspects of us that are split off or kept secret cannot be brought into resonant attuning, which is where we are vitalized. Perhaps partially embracing Desire leads to a life of form instead of substance.

Clearly, we cannot willfully make ourselves whole, but we can willingly allow our Desire to awaken us to our unhealthy behaviors. We can willingly allow our Desire to give us the confidence to name our secondary incentives for good to a trusted other. Then the resonant attuning of relationship readies us for the next step in healing.

Step 3: Accepting: accepting acknowledgment of our secondary incentives for good by the trusted other.

Why do we need to accept acknowledgment? Accepting moves us to the side of our trusted other so that together we can deal with the ways that distorted Desire results in distorted ways of connecting with others. Standing side by side while looking at the consequences of our behavior helps to maintain an attitude of valuing while we face what is shame-laden. Remember Jeremy's patient, Fred, whom we met in chapter 5? Once Fred could look at his participation in a swindle from Jeremy's viewpoint, he could see that he was trying to do the right thing. He wanted to meet another person and feel connected.

Jeremy, by not denying or excusing Fred's shameful behavior, invited him to look honestly at what he had done. At the same time that he held Fred in resonant attuning, Jeremy stood with him in his sense of shame as Fred questioned, "How could I have done such a thing?" Simultaneously, Jeremy clarified that the patient's shameful deed—his swindle—came out of his goodness in wanting a relationship. But his choice of relationship—his choice of a con man—derived from distorted Desire.

Fred's many inauthentic relationships left him starving for loving connections. His hunger allowed him to be swept up in the illusion of resonant attuning that the con man created. The con man operated not from his sacred Desire; he manipulated a false sense of resonance instead of sharing in genuine mutuality. Such inauthentic living can feel good for a time, but ultimately it does not satisfy our Desire.

Accepting Jeremy's acknowledgment of his distorted behavior began to free Fred from overwhelming shame. It freed him to realize what he had done and to take responsibility for it. It freed him to begin trusting his Desire. In so doing he began living his life less burdened by his inner "shoulds" and less in need of antidepressants to control his moods.

Our actual traumas and losses in life do not necessarily determine whether we live in resonant or dissonant attuning with our Desire; how we process these experiences does. The stories we construct about our life experiences determine how fully we live in resonance with our Desire. When this patient processed his life experiences within dissonant attuning with the parents in his memory, he sidetracked himself from his Desire. Being sidetracked, he was so hungry for relationship that he could be manipulated. When he processed his experience with the con man within resonant attuning with Jeremy, he reconnected with his sacred Desire. Within resonant attuning, he could tolerate looking at the damage he had caused without being pulled back into a state of shame.

Authentic living is living in harmony with our Desire.[4] Indeed, when we are authentic, we don't just feel good—we are good and our Desire motivates us to continue being good. We suggest that this motivation is mediated by the release of oxytocin, which generates the release of more oxytocin (See "The Holy Nectar," page 5).

When we accept acknowledgment of our distorted behavior, we can trust that our sacred Desire urges us to be good. Then we are free to repent.

Step 4: Repenting: allowing ourselves to be sorry for our distorted Desire and its behavioral consequences and allowing ourselves to be changed.

Allowing ourselves to feel sorry does not mean blaming ourself. It is realizing that when we live in our secondary incentives for good, we diminish ourself and others. We heard how Jeremy's patient, Fred, shamed his self by participating in a swindle. We saw how competition led to trampling a woman in the shopping blitz.

Living in secondary incentives, we also impede the vitality of our Desire. A story from Nancy's childhood illustrates how we starve our Desire when we live in secondary incentives and how repenting restores it and us.

In 1951, the Colorado Gold Rush seemed very close and very real to me and my cousin Mikey. I was five and he was six. We never missed a western movie. The mountains of our rural Colorado town were visible from the drive-in movie theater before it was dark enough to start the movie. A robbery, often of freshly mined gold, required action from one of our cowboy heroes. We would play out these stories day after day, over and over again until the next movie offered some new characters. We were children delighted to have each other to share in imagination.

Before his mother Maxine—my father's kid sister—and Mikey came to live with us, Mikey had suffered many losses. Mikey's step-father, Rudy, was sent to Korea for a tour of duty. Our grandfather, with whom they had been living, died suddenly of a heart attack. Mikey's real father, rumored to be a n'er-do-well, remained shrouded in mystery by the entire family.

At five I only dimly understood these family complexities. Sometimes I saw Mikey cry over our grandfather's death. But I hadn't known Grandfather well enough to feel much sadness of my own. And sometimes I saw my father's sadness. But most of the time Mikey and I enjoyed playing together for hours. Our companionship negated our usual loneliness of being only children.

At that time my parents rented a small house on the property of Marcia and Charlie Young. The Youngs lived in a beautiful new house on their "peach ranch." We knew to be careful crossing the road and to stay away from Charlie's very ill tempered donkey. It was also best to stay away from Charlie who didn't care much for young children interrupting his pruning, cultivating, and irrigating. Finally we knew to stay away from my grandmother on her too frequent visits, lest we get scolded for behaviors that didn't upset our parents. Because Grandmother clung to a punitive God, she was a creative theologian who took issue with noise, less than perfectly clean hands, our interest in cowboys and cattle rustlers, and our ignorance of Bible stories.

Marcia, a wonderful gardener, maintained the outside of her house with great care. Mikey and I had strict orders to stay out of her flowerbeds. That didn't cause a problem because we had no interest in pansies, roses or any other flowers; but we did have a fascination with some of Marcia's special rocks, particularly the ones that contained flecks of real Colorado gold. In terms of money, the rocks had little value, but for Mikey and me they were concrete proof that John Wayne, Roy Rogers, and Gene Autry could not be far away and that our games of cowboys and gold robberies had a real world basis.

Mikey realized that our time together was approaching an end before I did. Rudy returned home and plans were being made. Mikey began fighting with his mother over everything from what he had to wear to school to how he wanted to stay in Colorado. He didn't want to go back to California because his grandfather wasn't there anymore, but that seemed to be what was in store. It got harder to interest Mikey in gold robberies.

After weeks of agony, the day of their departure arrived. Rudy's Chevrolet was packed, and we were all up early to eat breakfast together. It must have been a Sunday because both my parents were home and my grandmother arrived to take me to Sunday school. Mikey and I were gloomy and moving as slowly as we could to try to make time stand still.

Then came a knock on the door. There stood Marcia, her usual cheerful smile replaced by a serious look. She announced, "Some of my 'gold' rocks are missing." All eyes but mine turned toward Mikey. Adults have an uncanny way of knowing things. I assumed some of those bad guys really did come to steal the gold. But they seemed to know immediately that Mikey was the culprit. All the adults intuitively knew that Mikey had stolen the "gold."

For now let's interrupt this story to look at Mikey's distorted Desire and its behavioral consequence—his theft. Mikey was losing relationships and didn't know how to handle his losses. Seemingly no one understood how frightened and sad he was as the loss of those he loved in Colorado reminded him of earlier losses that could never be restored to him. Holding onto the "gold," the last and most desperate of his several attempts to focus attention on his feelings, was a wake-up call for the seven people surrounding him. It said, "If you won't give me what I desire, I'll take it."

But Mikey misunderstood Desire. He thought he wanted the "gold." What he really wanted was the relationships. He wanted to stay in Colorado with Marcia and Charlie, with his mother and Nancy. How often do we commonly misunderstand Desire when we are hurting? How often do our unmet needs and frustrated Desire create in us a sense of desperation that demands action and twists our thinking?

Stealing gave Mikey a sense of power in being able to do something. According to his thinking the "gold" represented something of value. How often have we, like Mikey, lost faith about finding comfort in people and turned to objects for solace? How often has reaching for solace voiced our Desire?

Mikey desperately wanted everyone to know what he was feeling. He verbally expressed his wish to stay in Colorado. He fought with his mother. He lost interest in playing out gold robberies. Finally, his Desire for someone to resonantly attune to his feelings exploded as stealing the "gold" from Marcia's garden. The people in his environment shaped the expression of his Desire by their lack of understanding him. But even in theft, Mikey's Desire expressed itself. Getting caught stealing signaled to him and to those surrounding him that his Desire was going unmet.

How can we come to understand our sacred Desire correctly? How can we trust that our Desire is good? How can we surrender to the Divine within us? All of these questions get at the heart of the same mystery. Each uses a different language. *Desire* is the language of spirituality; *good* is the language of morality; *divine* is the language of theology. Were we to use love, we would be using the language of emotions. But all get at the same mystery of our essential nature. Imbedded in our desire for human relationships lives our Desire for the Divine. In the words of the Doctor of Desire, Pope Gregory the Great, "The very 'desire' is what gives us pleasure, not just its gratification."[5]

Let us resume Mikey's story and see how trusting our Desire shapes our being. Remember where we left Mikey? With seven people staring at him, he knew that they knew that he did it.

> It didn't take long for him to confess that he had stolen the gold. His confession surprised and hurt me because he had left me out of his plan.
>
> Mikey managed to explain that he took the gold so that he could buy a ticket in California and return to Colorado. It may have seemed like a tall tale, but it would have been easier for Mikey had they accused him of making up the story. Instead my dad and Rudy made Mikey's pain much worse by smiling and jeering at him. "Don't you know that those 'gold' rocks aren't worth more than a few cents?" I knew this mockery cut Mikey to the quick.
>
> Adding insult to injury, my grandmother immediately began to berate him, "How could you do something as terrible as stealing? And how could you do this to someone who has been so kind to you? How can anyone ever trust you? This is a very bad sign of what will become of you in the future." "Blood is thicker than water," she reminded us. The ghostly presence of Mikey's real father suddenly seemed alive in the room.
>
> By now Mikey had collapsed in tears. His feeble attempts to deny and then explain his theft had given way to sobs. I started to cry too. My dad's and Rudy's jeering and my grandmother's blaming hurt both Mikey and me. Frustration mounted. Now I, my grandmother, my dad, Rudy, and Mikey were all in a state of despair. We felt the "badness" within ourselves that my grandmother accused Mikey of.
>
> Fortunately Mikey's story did not end with my grandmother's and the men's responses to him. A voice of wisdom broke into the scene.

Marcia, the so-called injured party, said that she didn't think Mikey was a criminal. "Yes, he had taken the rocks with the gold on them, but not to be bad. He took the rocks so he could come back and be with us. Even if the rocks weren't worth enough to pay for a trip back, they would be a way he tried to hold onto all of us."

Marcia suggested that Mikey show her where he packed the rocks. The two of them went with Rudy to open the back seat and move Mikey's comic books. There they were, the muddy earth starting to dry. Marcia and Mikey carried the four or five rocks to the flower bed and replaced them in their tell-tale empty places.

Marcia assured Mikey that he was always welcome to come back. It had been a good year for all of us, and she understood that he liked the rocks with gold in them; she did, too. We had become friends, and it is hard for friends to part.

I have never forgotten that day of parting because it stirred such strong feelings in me. I felt both the squelching of my vitality by those who judged Mikey as "bad" and also the restoration of my vitality by Marcia who valued Mikey as "good."

Grandmother's morality was judgmental as was Dad's and Rudy's. Their jeering essentially said, "If you're going to steal, steal what is worth something. As a man you should know the value of the object. Or, don't get caught." Their berating Mikey attempted to end Mikey's childish stealing with the use of their adult verbal punishment. Instead, their judging violated his being by diverting him into feeling he was "bad."

Marcia attuned differently from Grandmother, Dad, and Rudy. She named Mikey's theft, which led to a process that prevented him from leaving as a thief. But she named his deed without blaming and with resonant attuning to his hurting about having to leave. Marcia's response was a refreshing invitation for Mikey and us to experience more clearly our pain of separation. Her trust in the goodness of Mikey's Desire to hold onto those he loved not only restored Mikey's vitality; it also restored the vitality of all who could receive her valuing. It shaped our being into feeling we were "good." It changed our minds and spirits; it restructured our brains; it turned us from our Second Nature to our First Nature.

How often do we wittingly or unwittingly judge others or ourselves in an attempt to make us better people? To stop judging calls us to live in the consequences of the choices we make in life. It frees us to see how we attune and to take responsibility for how our attuning affects others and us. Knowing when we've caused hurt, we naturally experience regret, sorrow, or grief.

Marcia could experience sorrow because she lived in a state that allowed her to resonantly attune to Mikey's pain. In relationships of resonant attuning, love and valuing prevail. Love, here, is an ability to stand with the other person in his or her pain. Her resonant attuning to Mikey's suffering repaired the damage done by the dissonant attuning of Nancy's grandmother, her dad, and Rudy. It drew everyone into Mikey's suffering so that they could deal with it. Their suffering together freed Mikey to embrace Marcia as valuing him, to experience himself as good, to be sorry for his stealing, and to repent.

We are always in need of repentance. In this life we never finally get over the dissonant attuning gaze of our parents and each other. We promise our self not ever again to behave from distorted Desire, but again we do so. Yet when we do it again, we do it not as the same person we were or in the same way. The fact that we are always in need of repentance is why we have both mothers and fathers, both grandmothers and "Marcias" so that when one decreases our vitality the other can restore us. With restored vitality, our Desire—like Mikey's—invites us to face forgiveness.

Step 5: Forgiving: establishing and sustaining resonant attuning, which changes us and allows us to forgive the person with whom we've had a dissonant attuning relationship and to live into the forgiveness of ourselves for the consequences of our actions.

Healing may or may not involve forgiveness by the person with whom we were dissonantly attuning. It may be a third person— therapist, clergy, or friend—who pronounces forgiveness. But true healing must ultimately involve our forgiveness of that person. It must also involve our living into the forgiveness of our self that has been pronounced by another, often the most difficult step.

Forgiving is not a matter of following a set of steps. It is a complex process that involves bringing into being new expectations for our self and for our relationships, a process that changes us (our mind, spirit, brain, and very physiology) by changing our memories. Our memories are living flesh. By establishing and sustaining resonant attuning, we change the memories we made in dissonant attuning. In so doing, changing our memories changes our flesh. Once we are no longer entrapped in the flesh of dissonance, we see differently.

Once we live in the flesh of resonance, forgiveness happens. Then we can compassionately and genuinely forgive the other with whom we developed our distortedness. Then we can live into our own forgiveness.

Sally's patient, Barbara, shows us what it means to surrender to Desire's healing power. Barbara also shows us how resonant attuning to our sacred Desire changes us so that forgiveness can happen.

> As I was leaving Pinetree Clinic after seeing patients all day, Barbara appeared. Without calling for an appointment, she just walked into the clinic. Disheveled and desperate-looking, I quickly found out that she was suicidal. Since I happened to be on call that evening, Barbara consented to meet me in the psychiatric emergency room where I was headed.
>
> The emergency room staff and I took a great deal of time with Barbara. We learned that she was a very respected executive for a major business firm. She had long suffered from depression, with one serious suicide attempt that had resulted in hospitalization ten years earlier. Memories of that hospitalization—where she had felt misunderstood and humiliated—haunted Barbara.
>
> Because she had been reared to rely on herself, Barbara's accomplishments in the career world confirmed for her that she needed no

one. Being able to take care of herself served as a powerful secondary incentive for maintaining her self-esteem. Her current depression, however, threatened this cherished strategy. Barbara reacted to the threat by acquiring a stash of cyanide sufficient to kill herself. She would take care of herself even if it meant ending her life!

Despite the time we spent with her, Barbara was too afraid to enter the hospital voluntarily. I decided to respect her fear as long as she would promise to see me the next day. Barbara and I got through one day at a time. After a week of such effort, it was clear to both of us that her depression was so severe that neither she nor I could manage it without additional help. Barbara needed hospitalization for two weeks to protect her until a new antidepressant medication worked and until experiences of resonant attuning could be established. She allowed me to walk her to the hospital that was near my office. There I admitted her.

Admission to a psychiatric hospital challenged Barbara's view of herself as self-sufficient and stirred the frightening memories of her previous hospitalization. Because her previous hospitalization primed her to expect a similar painful experience, I decided to mediate Barbara's experience with the hospital staff.

My mediation was a careful effort to show Barbara and the staff their interdependence. One day, for example, Barbara misplaced her glasses. Staff, without thought, imposed a hospital rule that patients not use the phone during activity time and refused her request to call a friend to bring her another pair. On another occasion, Barbara developed a migraine and experienced difficulty convincing the staff of her pain. When Barbara complained to me about the staff, she and I acknowledged Barbara's feeling misunderstood and her feeling controlled by staff "for her own good," but neither of us retaliated by angrily accusing the staff. We acknowledged all real or perceived shortcomings of the system while simultaneously acknowledging the strengths of the system. That is, the system would protect Barbara from killing herself until her mood improved despite any shortcomings in herself or in the staff.

I worked similarly with the hospital staff. When the staff complained, "Barbara's treating us as though we're bad," I encouraged them to address their reactions including their fears that Barbara might not get well and might subsequently commit suicide. This allowed staff to live more from their Desire to value Barbara in her wholeness (in both her strengths and her weaknesses) and not get sidetracked into either devaluing Barbara out of their fears for Barbara's life or retaliating out of their conviction that Barbara's "bad" conduct needed punishment. Most important, staff members were able to acknowledge that they were good enough to provide a healing environment if they believed in their goodness.

Barbara grew from a frightened, suicidal, and highly defensive patient who initially experienced the insults of others as rejection into a woman who was able to understand both the shortcomings and also the concerns that others felt for her. Not only Barbara but also all of us profited from accepting our fears rather than retaliating. All of us profited from sustaining a belief in our own goodness and in the adequacy of our goodness. We awakened to the best within us and found original solutions within our evolving relationships. Barbara, for example, surrendered her stash of cyanide; the staff graciously received it in a formal ceremony; I rejoiced with them.

When Barbara agreed to move from inpatient to partial hospitalization, the staff welcomed her. As a result of their positive cycle of interactions, Barbara returned to health. Accepting her vulnerability and her need for others vitalized her relationships in the hospital and revitalized her personal relationships outside the hospital. For example, her troubled relationship with her mother changed dramatically. Barbara's mother had never been able to value her or to meet her needs. As a result, Barbara got sidetracked from trusting others into needing no one. "I can take care of myself" became her motto.

In outpatient psychotherapy as she re-experienced, within resonant attuning with me, the pain of her mother's dissonant attuning and the frustration of never meeting her mother's expectations, she could accept her own vulnerability to pain and her mother's shortcomings. Ultimately, she realized that she could forgive her mother while not denying the dissonant attuning that her mother brought to their relationship.

Forgiveness took place when Barbara experienced things differently. By not fighting against surrender, but by remembering the dissonant attuning experiences that resulted in her feeling so vulnerable, she reclaimed her integrity. Authentic forgiveness resulted from her awareness of the pain of dissonant attuning and from her tolerance of the loss of illusions about herself such as the false belief that she needed no one. Authentic forgiveness reflected the conviction that the recovery of trust is possible and that love can be recreated and maintained in spite of and beyond her vulnerability.

Professor David Augsburger, in his book *Helping People Forgive,* tells us what forgiveness is not.[6] Forgiveness is not excusing. Barbara held staff, her mother, herself, and me accountable for our behavior. Forgiveness is not forgetting. Dissonant attuning had happened and was written permanently into her brain. But Barbara changed the meaning of the dissonance from "rejection" to "shortcomings." Forgiveness is not necessarily reconciling. When the other is an unrepentant chronic abuser, separation is sometimes necessary for physical and psychological survival. But separation is not sufficient for forgiveness. Forgiveness still requires a change in attitude toward the now-absent other. Forgiveness took Barbara's strength to accept in her heart a person (her mother) who was responsible for hurting her. Forgiveness is not condoning or tolerating. Barbara did not overlook or ignore her mother's dissonant attuning. She forgave what she could not condone or tolerate. Forgiveness is not the same as *feeling* loving; it is the same as loving, which is rooted in volition—the will to do good, the will to work for good for another. Forgiveness must be honest. It cannot be forced. Forgiveness happens if we allow it. It can happen quickly or it can take years.

Just as being sorry was not blaming herself, forgiveness was neither blaming herself nor blaming her mother. Forgiveness healed the relationship between Barbara and her mother. In Barbara's words, "I am now the daughter my mother always wanted and my mother is the mother I always wanted."

Bringing new expectations into her being and into her relationship with her mother was a joyous process; letting go of old expectations was a grieving process. Grieving was occasioned by her shattering encounter with truth: "Mother always thwarts my needs." It began with mourning the loss of denial, denial of that truth. It continued as mourning the loss of beliefs that she understandably created from denial of that truth but that disconnected her from her sacred Desire, which was "I yearn for relationship." And grieving involved mourning the loss of her secondary incentive for good, which was "I am self-sufficient." All her grieving was part of dying to her Second Nature. It was very painful.

Grief took Barbara into her own depth where she could ask herself: What fear provoked my self-deceit that I did not need my mother? Was I afraid I would totally alienate and lose her? Was I afraid I would lose her love or approval? Was I afraid of her retaliation? She answered, "No, but I did feel ashamed about not living up to my own internal standard of being self-sufficient, and, therefore, I hid from myself behind a lie of needing no one."

Acknowledging her shame disclosed the expectation of being thwarted by her mother's dissonant attuning. The permanence of her expectation was determined by the fact that she had experienced dissonant attuning very early in life and with the person who was emotionally most important to her.

Barbara gave up grievances and accepted grief. When she remembered in order to forgive rather than to retaliate, she remembered in order to take responsibility and cooperate with her healing. Had she remembered in order to retaliate, she would have remembered in order to destroy the relationship with her mother, and in so doing she would have attacked the very source of her repair, which was a relationship within resonant attuning.

This is what Barbara began to achieve when she surrendered to her fears about hospitalization and to her fears about depending on others. Experiencing a state of resonant attuning with me allowed her to stay with her fears without retaliating. This reconnected her with her sacred Desire, where she was freed up to be different and, hence, to behave differently. She gave up her cyanide and forgave her mother.

Step 6: Choosing our Desire for resonant attuning: choosing life.

Sustained resonance moves us from brokenness and blame to an acceptance that the violation of relationship came from mutual brokenness. Now the forgiving person can intentionally live more fully in First Nature and journey from fear back to love.

This is what Barbara did when she learned to welcome her Desire. Resonantly attuning to her Desire changed her and those with whom she related. We might say that Barbara spiritually surrendered to Desire. Spiritual surrender is reaching for Desire, surrendering to that which is wholly trustworthy. It is surrender to a hope and trust that a life-giving relationship is possible. It is choosing life.

In his book *Will and Spirit,* the late psychiatrist Gerald May delineates six criteria for discerning the legitimacy of spiritual surrender:[7]

Spiritual surrender is *conscious.* Barbara was fully aware of everything that was happening at the time she decided to enter the hospital, at the time she gave her stash of cyanide to the hospital staff, and at the time she decided she could forgive her mother without forgetting her mother's dissonant attuning.

Spiritual surrender is *intentional.* Barbara freely chose. No one coerced her nor did she compel herself. She willingly gave herself.

Spiritual surrender is a *responsible act.* Should her decisions have been a mistake, Barbara was prepared to accept responsibility for her decisions.

Spiritual surrender also involves *responsibility for the consequences* as well as responsibility for the act. Barbara did not blame the staff when she felt misunderstood or mistreated. She accepted their shortcomings and took responsibility for hers.

Spiritual surrender is *not directed toward any fully known "object."* Barbara did not fully know her Desire for resonant attuning. Yet, surrendering to her Desire was taking her own mysterious soul and resonantly attuning it to the Ultimate Mystery that had created and energized it.

Spiritual surrendering represents a *willingness to engage the fullness of life with the fullness of oneself.* Barbara's spiritual surrender was not a means for furthering her self-importance. It was not an escape or an avoidance. It was a "yes" rather than a "no" to the decisions she made.

Often our ongoing relationships remain difficult despite all our efforts. We see that our rational arguments threaten the very ways of thinking that keep the other feeling secure. One alternative is to remain in the relationship and bear witness to more loving ways of relating, hoping to bring about change in the other and in the relationship.

When change seems impossible, how do we decide to stay or to leave? First we ask ourselves—perhaps with the help of another—many questions, including: Am I staying because I'm afraid of change? Am I staying due to failure of optimism that a better relationship is possible? The questions will vary depending on the individual. If we do leave and find a relationship that is not threatened by our presence and that reciprocally nourishes us, then we can live to make alternative ways of relating available for all people.

Our minds and brains and spirits continue to grow throughout our development into and through adulthood, where maturation invites continuing reorganization of our attuning experiences. As long as we are alive, the Desire for resonance is within us. This is the healing power of Desire. Though it is not all we mean by redemption—as we will see in the next chapter—the healing power of Desire is a particular embodied example of what redemption is like. Barbara's Desire was indomitable. Her healing restored hope and trust that had been undermined by dissonant attuning experiences. She turned from fear (Desire that is sidetracked from love) back to love (Desire that is aligned with love).

The pivotal moment in Barbara's life was the "now moment." The now moment is a concept coined by psychiatrist and infant researcher Daniel Stern. It refers to a moment in the present that suddenly arises "as an emergent property of the moving along process."[8] The now moment creates a crisis that needs a resolution. Resolution can occur as an interpretation or as a moment of meeting—a moment when two people become aware of what each other is experiencing.

The now moment for Barbara was her walking into the Pinetree Clinic at a time when I was not as intent on going home as I might have been had I finished my day. Because I was not finished, I spent more time with her than I otherwise might have. The now moment allowed Barbara to get a feel for the person—me—whom she would see in the emergency room. I doubt that she would have gone to the emergency room had I referred her there to meet someone entirely unknown.

The crisis that the now moment created was a crisis of awareness. Could we both take the time to become aware of what her unannounced appearance showed us? Our mutual recognition of her desperation was our "moment of meeting" that opened our mutual awareness to how needy she was. Our moment of meeting led ultimately to Barbara's reliving within the resonant attuning of hospital staff and me her painful past memories that had been made in dissonant attuning. Changing those memories by reliving them within resonant attuning freed Barbara to experience herself as the child her mother always wanted and to experience her mother as the mother Barbara always wanted.

In sum, Barbara's insecure attachment bond to her mother got imprinted in her brain during childhood (See "Attachment Patterns," page 36). She lived from that model, which she brought into all her adult relationships. When that model got her into trouble, she fortunately came into my clinic. Within the resonant attuning relationship of our encounter, the "now moment" emerged as an invitation to live life differently.

The good news is that the "now moment" can happen at any time in any relationship in everyday life. This is our invitation to realize that our Desire is alive and we can trust its urge. We can live in resonant attuning, where our Desire animates and transforms us and our relationships.

Step 7: Transforming: embracing, and being embraced by the Holy.

The sensation of transformation is commonly described as a rebirth—being born of the spirit. Rebirth means freedom from the bondage of secondary incentives for good and the renewal of our primary incentive for good. Transformation frees our Desire from its association with fear and shame. This brings us again to the fear of our goodness.

One day we authors stumbled upon a quotation from Marianne Williamson's *A Return to Love* that Nelson Mandela included in his comments when he was inaugurated as president of the new, free Republic of South Africa on May 10, 1994:

> Our deepest fear is not that we are inadequate. Our deepest fear is that we are powerful beyond measure. It is our light, not our darkness, that most frightens us. . . . You are a child of God. Your playing small doesn't serve the world. There's nothing enlightened about shrinking so that other people won't feel insecure around you. We are all meant to shine, as children do. We were born to manifest the glory of God [the Divine] that is within us. It's not just in some of us; it's in everyone. And as we let our own light shine, we unconsciously give other people permission to do the same. As we are liberated from our own fear, our presence automatically liberates others.[9]

The provocative notion that what human beings fear most is our light caused us to pause. We pondered this question: Is it true that human beings are most afraid of their light?

We wondered why Nelson Mandela would choose to read these particular words of Williamson, words about the goodness of humanity, and so we began to learn about his journey. The youngest son of thirteen black African children and the first of his family ever to attend school, Mandela became one of the great moral and political leaders of the twentieth century. When Mandela was born in 1918, his father, a counselor for the rulers of his South African tribe, named him Rolihlahla, which colloquially means "troublemaker." As was the custom in that white-ruled country, Rolihlahla's teacher gave him a new name, Nelson, on his first day at school. Nelson Mandela devoted his life to establishing racial equality in South Africa. That commitment led to the honor of being elected president of the Republic of South Africa at the age of seventy-six and to his receiving the Nobel Peace Prize in 1993. But prior to those honors, he served many long, hard years in prison.

Imprisonment objectifies and humiliates human beings, and in Mandela's situation his jailers undoubtedly held the power to take his life. Yet after two and one-half decades in prison, where he must have experienced and witnessed the extremes of human cruelty, Mandela emerged to endorse the basic light in all people. Only a most remarkable person could sustain or evolve a belief in basic human goodness under those circumstances.

Did Mandela see that the cruelty of human beings resulted from their deep fear of their basic goodness? Did he see that his jailers' cruelty arose from fear not only of Mandela's goodness but also fear of their own?

The words that Mandela selected to read at his inauguration inspired us to search our own hearts for our deepest fear. If our deepest fear is of the power of our goodness, might this fear lead us to hide our goodness from others and ourselves and to act without awareness of our inner light? Is it fear of our goodness that leads us to lose touch with our sacred Desire, which is the very essence of our being?

As Mandela explained to Oprah Winfrey and all her television viewers, he was able to connect with his inner goodness because he connected with a larger vision of the goodness of all people. Mandela's connection with a vision of the goodness of all people must have enabled him to connect with people experiencing brokenness. Apparently connecting with goodness strengthened him so that when he resonantly attuned to the broken spirit of an oppressed victim, he did not succumb to the victim's brokenness. Apparently he could also resonantly attune to the angry fury of a humiliated victim without rising up in self-righteous indignation. We posit that he did not fear his own goodness because his Desire was not distorted by being associated with shame.

Mandela must have faced several choices. When oppressed, he could have chosen to believe the white man's claim that he deserved imprisonment, or, when released from prison, he could have chosen to retaliate and kill his oppressors. These solutions would have locked him into continuing oppression, both of himself and others. Instead, Mandela chose to recognize his own and all people's sameness: we all do bad things but we are also—all of us—good.

This recognition required the ability to transcend and see beyond the prison walls, literal and metaphysical, of South African society. The metaphysical walls were walls of fear. From his own experience Mandela must have known that once free from fear, everyone, as he had, could live in a different reality and could create a different world. Also from his own experience, he must have known that reclaiming goodness was dangerous. The power of goodness repeatedly threatened all whose vested interest lay in maintaining oppression. Their fear had led them to imprison Mandela and his friends. But Mandela apparently knew that to free the oppressed, the oppressors also must be freed. All must be freed from their fears.

You and I are not Nelson Mandela, but we—like him—face the challenge of good and evil in the world. We have the opportunity to embrace "our light, not our darkness." We can choose to embrace the light of others, not their darkness.

Now we ask: Dare we *not* believe what Marianne Williamson asserts and what Nelson Mandela's life demonstrates? Dare we not treat ourself and others as living subjective parts of one nature? Dare we not attune to the universe and see ourselves forming one unity with others? Dare we not awaken our own deepest most authentic light?

Knowing people who have lived life from their sacred Desire helps. First, they inspire us. Nelson Mandela inspired us authors; Mahatma Gandhi inspired Nelson Mandela. Second, they instruct us. Nelson Mandela taught us that when dissonant attuning occurred, he managed his reactions to it by recognizing them, by owning them, by seeking reparation with those whose attuning was dissonant, and by re-establishing resonant attuning when possible. Third, they show us by example. Mandela showed us how managing his reactions of aggression transformed them from vengeance into love. Managing his reactions of fear transformed them from retaliation to joy and peace. Mandela's life stirred our courage to enter the process ourselves.

What we learned—personally and professionally, scientifically and spiritually—is that fostering the Light of others fosters our Light; fostering the good of others fosters our good. In this regard, the question of our identity is a moral question. We are determined by our Desire to attune to our inner Light, which is the Divine within us. If we deny our Desire, we prevent ourselves from seeing our own and others' Light. Satisfying our sacred Desire gives permission for others to satisfy their sacred Desire. As Nelson Mandela quoted Marianne Williamson, "We were born to manifest the glory of God [the Divine] that is within us. It's not just in some of us; it's in everyone."

CHAPTER 8

REDEMPTIVE ATTUNING

Desire's Continuing Journey

> The moment of meeting with the old man had been
> like the opening of a door; through it he had moved
> into a new dimension of life, where the world itself
> and all experience and action within it had sacra-
> mental value.
>
> —ELIZABETH GOUDGE

D ESIRE'S JOURNEY does not end with healing. By repairing some of the distortions to our sacred Desire, healing prepares us for a qualitatively different journey: a journey into redemptive attuning. In this continuing journey of Desire, we live more of the time in a transformed First Nature, where biologically and psychologically our sacred Desire is safer. We are still attuning when we live in a transformed First Nature because that is who we are. But we live from a more secure biological and psychological foundation, where we use our brain mirror neurons to attune to each other with resonance, where we co-create each other in a physiology of love, and where we share joy that animates our sacred Desire for the holy. From this firmer psychological and biological foundation, our sacred Desire spiritually flows more freely. Although we still suffer when we encounter dissonance, we are not so easily trapped in dissonant attuning. Indeed, living in a state of redemptive attuning frees us to suffer with compassion, which protects our sacred Desire from distortion.

When our sacred Desire is freer, we experience the world as a gift intended to draw us into enjoying each other, all of creation, and the Creator of all. In a state of redemptive attuning, to use the words of Elizabeth Goudge, sacred Desire moves us "into a new dimension of life, where the world itself and all experience and action within it [has] sacramental value."[1] In such an understanding of the world, we delight in each and all things as messages to us from the Creator. Everyone and everything is a sacrament, a sign of the truth that our minds seek and a sign of the communion that our spirits yearn for. Everyone and everything share in a reality where God (the Divine) is manifest.

Mark McIntosh, associate professor of systematic theology and spirituality at Loyola University of Chicago, says,

> creation is, in truth, suffused by the radiant ever-more of its Creator and can only be perceived truly by those who are themselves attuned to that ever-sharing 'more' of divine life. In this sense creation is intrinsically signful . . . and can only be understood and known as it is read . . . in tandem with the divine reality that give rise to it.[2]

What happens to us when we live in redemptive attuning? Most simply, sacred Desire carries us into a process of radical internal change where all of our aspects—biological, psychological, sociocultural, and spiritual—are restored to love, to our First Nature. But, restored to our First Nature, we are not the same person we used to be. We are more compassionate, have more humility, and exercise more freedom to step out of our automatic Second Nature reactions that were created in dissonant attuning. We can now understand our automatic Second Nature reactions with resonant attuning and begin to change them.

Something important distinguishes redemptive attuning from

Spiritual Development

Ages	Consciousness Level[a]	Attuning[b]
Infancy (0–1 ½)		0–2 months: Emergent self = body self
		Innate ability to enter into the other's experience and participate in it
		2–6 months: Core self
		Affect attuning: sharing inner feeling states
		6–9 months: Subjective self
	1–3 years: Archaic consciousness	12 months: Social referencing is seen
	Child's body is separate from mother's and others' bodies	Attuning gives rise to empathy
		15–18 months: Verbal self
	Child's emotions are separate from mother's and others' emotions	Can grasp the intentions of others
		Attuning to how others see us elicits the moral emotion of shame
Early childhood (2–6)	2–7 years: Magical consciousness	3–5 years: Narrative self
	The outside world revolves around the self	By 5 has a more formal capacity to represent mental states of self and others by combining cognition and resonance
		Attuning gives rise to the developmental achievement of guilt

Childhood (7–12)	7–12 years: Mythic consciousness	
	The child learns to define itself by conventional rules and roles and sees its self-worth in following the "laws" and behaving properly	
Adolescence (13–21)	13–21 years: Rational consciousness	
	Can think abstractly and grasp universal principles	
	Average adult attains this	
Young Adulthood (21–35) Adulthood (35–60) Maturity (60–)	Vision-logic consciousness (some adults) Can take many different perspectives, integrate them, and put them together in new ways	Self transformed by love from blind to seeing Can attune to all and seek their good Attuning gives rise to the developmental achievement of remorse and *altruism*

Psychology tells us nothing beyond the vision-logic level where we can see and measure things. Spirituality says there is more. What follows is our understanding of spiritual development as it can develop over adulthood.

Sidebar continues

the psychological healing of individual or interpersonal vicious cycles. According to Professor of Theology David Kelsey, in redemption an element of grace appears. We agree with Professor Kelsey when grace is defined in the way that Saint Thérèse of Lisieux understood it: "not as something that God gives, but as the divine, loving presence at the core of her [our] being."[3] In other words,

Spiritual Development, *continued*

Ages	Consciousness Level[a]	Redemptive Attuning[c]
Adulthood (21–)	Psychic consciousness	Self revolves around a central axis, a "still-point"
	Identification with the inner witness, the still, small voice within	Can attune to the still, small voice within
	Subtle consciousness	Self identified with the Divine
	Inner identification with the Divine	Attuning to the Divine
	Divine consciousness	Self experiences union, oneness with the Divine
	Awareness of oneness with the Divine	Self sees the Divine in all things (immanent) and sees all things in the Divine (transcendent)
	Must translate intuitions into words	Attuning to joy
	Nondual consciousness	"That" in us that loves and is one with God is Christ (Christian)
	Dissolution of self-awareness (ecstasy)	Self disappears (Buddhist no-self)
		Identity of what Is (Hindu One Ultimate Existent)
		Attuning to the Unknown
	Being is doing The Divine and I are One	
	Fully human: The essence of man	*Fully realized altruism*

This is spiritual development after self disappears. It is the continuing journey of No-Self.

Falling away of Unity = No-Consciousness, No-Self[d]

Resurrection

The body (and all form) is Eternal Form
"knowing" that is beyond knower and known

Ascension

Body dissolves into "divine air."

The Divine is ALL Existence and EVERYWHERE: the
ultimate nature of man, his destiny

Incarnation

Eucharistic state: we share in the divinity of Christ as
Christ shared in our humanity

a. Derived from Jim Marion, *Putting on the Mind of Christ* (Charlottesville, Va.:
Hampton Roads Pub. Co., 2000).

b. Derived from Daniel N. Stern, *The Present Moment in Psychotherapy and
Everyday Life* (New York: W. W. Norton, 2004).

c. Derived from Bernadette Roberts, *The Experience of No-Self: A Contemplative
Journey* (Albany: State University of New York Press, 1993).

d. Derived from Bernadette Roberts, *What Is Self? A Study of the Spiritual Journey in Terms of Consciousness* (Boulder, Colo.: Sentient Publications, 2005).

Note: Although this chart presents spiritual development as linear, the process
seems to be spiral or nonlinear with an ebb and flow. It is possible to attune
to the Divine without ever moving smoothly through previous stages and to
reach vision-logic consciousness and beyond at an earlier age than the aver-
ages shown here.

Source: Nancy K. Morrison and Sally K. Severino, "Altruism: Toward a Psychobiospiritual Conceptualization," *Zygon: Journal of Religion and Science* 42, no. 1
(2007): 27–28.

redemption involves changes that "are not finally self-generated
nor evoked by interaction with other human beings; they are
grace, freely given from beyond the entire network of human
interactions."[4]

A paradox exists here. Redemption does indeed require us individually to engage with another in resonant attuning. But when
redemption occurs, it occurs not *solely* as a product of our self or of
our interrelatedness. It occurs by the release of something beyond

but within us, which is "the divine, loving presence at the core of our being." In redemptive attuning we are in harmony with the divine presence within us so that it can flow from us to others.

Why do we need grace? Because evil is real and powerful. The power of evil is not superior to the power of good, but because evil derives from within us—from within us when we are in our Second Nature—we are blind to it. When we live in our Second Nature, we live in a state of fear, which causes us to believe that our secondary incentives are good. This is true for all of us because we all carry within us states that were developed in unrepaired dissonant attuning. Left *solely* to our human interactions and logic, we remain stuck in these early established invariant neurobiological patterns that can be redeemed only by grace (the Divine) flowing through us.

Psychologist Jack Kornfield tells a poignant story that illustrates redemptive attuning.

> Once on the train from Washington to Philadelphia, I found myself seated next to an African-American man who'd worked for the State Department in India but had quit to run a rehabilitation program for juvenile offenders in the District of Columbia. Most of the youths he worked with were gang members who had committed homicide.
>
> One fourteen-year-old boy in his program had shot and killed an innocent teenager to prove himself to his gang. At the trial, the victim's mother sat impassively silent until the end, when the youth was convicted of the killing. After the verdict was announced, she stood up slowly and stared directly at him and stated, "I'm going to kill you." Then the youth was taken away to serve several years in the juvenile facility.
>
> After the first half year the mother of the slain child went to visit his killer. He had been living on the streets before the killing, and she was the only visitor he'd had. For a time they talked, and when she left she gave him some money for cigarettes. Then she started step by step to visit him more regularly, bringing food and small gifts. Near the end of his three-year sentence she asked him what he would be doing when he got out. He was confused and very uncertain, so she

offered to help set him up with a job at a friend's company. Then she inquired about where he would live, and since he had no family to return to, she offered him temporary use of the spare room in her home.

For eight months he lived there, ate her food, and worked at the job. Then one evening she called him into the living room to talk. She sat down opposite him and waited. Then she started, "Do you remember in the courtroom when I said I was going to kill you?" "I sure do," he replied. "I'll never forget that moment."

"Well, I did," she went on. "I did not want the boy who could kill my son for no reason to remain alive on this earth. I wanted him to die. That's why I started to visit you and bring you things. That's why I got you the job and let you live here in my house. That's how I set about changing you. And that old boy, he's gone. So now I want to ask you, since my son is gone, and that killer is gone, if you'll stay here. I've got room, and I'd like to adopt you if you let me." And she became the mother of her son's killer, the mother he never had.[5]

This mother shows us how redemptive attuning can break the vicious cycle of violence and revenge. Redemptive attuning involves loving one's enemies. In this case, the enemy was her son's killer whom she—with the help of grace—redeemed by her love. Love is not a soft and fuzzy anything-is-okay process. This mother neither denied the destructive violence of the killer nor demeaned the memory of her son by interfering with the killer's punishment. Her son's killer had committed a crime and needed to live in the consequences as part of his redemptive process.

Through redemptive attuning she stood with him in his pain each time she visited him in the juvenile facility. Essentially she embraced her son's killer. Simultaneously she must have embraced herself by standing in her own pain and anger about her son's death and by standing in her remorse about living in a society that produces gangs and killers. She did not allow her anger to hold her in the violence of hating her son's killer. Redemptive attuning allowed her to bear her suffering and to build a relationship with the boy. Evidently, within the redemptive attuning relationship, she was able to let go her animosities toward him and to respect him for who he was. He evidently was able to trust her enough to live with her despite her threat to kill him.

Once he entered her home, she continued loving him—forgiving him and willing his good—until the old boy was gone. Her threat to kill him can now be understood as the means by which redemptive attuning eliminates one's enemy but not with violence. Instead, she created and he participated in a relationship of redemptive attuning that transformed them both. Both underwent radical internal change. Then they could let the past be the past and redirect their creative energies to a fresh future. Their mutual tragedy became a coherent life narrative for both of them, which placed them in a new context, one freed from the bondage of Second Nature, which is the source of violence and vengeance.

Paradoxically, this mother and boy show us the virtue of fear. Until now we have looked at how attuning to those who frighten or threaten us distorts our Desire, causing us to act defensively out of fear rather than creatively out of love. We have talked about fear *of* goodness that we experience when we live in our Second Nature, where our sacred Desire has been met with dissonant attuning that remains unrepaired, resulting in our sacred Desire becoming distorted by fear/shame and becoming part of our self that is despised/enraged.

Now we turn to the virtue of fear—the fear that is at the heart of redemptive attuning. We call it "fear *for* goodness" to distinguish it from "fear *of* goodness." We experience it when we live in redeemed First Nature. When we grow into redeemed First Nature, we become increasingly aware that goodness can be harmed. As a result we fear *for* goodness, and we are concerned to maintain our goodness and the goodness of all. In other words, we fear *for* goodness because we now recognize that our sacred Desire and the sacred Desire of others can become distorted.

In developing this idea of fearing for and protecting our goodness, we can rely on the teachings of Buddhism, which show us how to transform destructive emotions like fear and anger in order to actualize our fundamental goodness.[6] We can also draw upon the thinking of twentieth-century iconoclast Ivan Illich. In his and David Cayley's book, *The Rivers North of the Future*, Illich devotes an entire chapter to the virtue of fear. He begins his argument by distinguishing two kinds of fear: *timor filialis*—a child's fear that he might allow something to interfere between him and his parent, and *timor servilis*—a servant's fear of being beaten. We would see *timor filialis* as the fear of the child who lives in First Nature and fears allowing something to interfere with the resonant attuning between him and his parents. *Timor servilis* is the fear of someone living in Second Nature who fears punishment.

Illich explains:

> Servile fear and filial fear are interdependent on a very deep level. I need to know that my offence was personal, my ingratitude was personal, the disappointment which I produced was personal, and ought not to be eliminated by running to confession or to a psychologist or psychiatrist. Only if I have a *vis-à-vis* who insists, "Son, you offend me," can I live in constant watchfulness not to let anything come between me and the other who passes by. Such watchfulness requires this foundation of fear and trembling.[7]

Illich claims that the fear—that I might break our relationship—got changed in Western societies during the twelfth century when the Christian Church redefined sin as a legal rather than a personal offense. This criminalization of sin gave shape to the fear of hell or other diabolical fantasies that became prominent in the fourteenth century. Furthermore, Illich says that in our time fear has changed its quality again. It is not the devil but technology that is the darkness that makes a sham of our freedom—technology with its risk management, its Prozac, its prison systems, and all its other systems that function to satisfy our perceived needs and to diminish our personal encounter.

All of these fears have arisen as we have disembodied ourselves. The original purpose of our bodies, of our senses, was a natural spiritual function, but the function of our eyes has been impoverished by technology. Technology creates an illusion of making life easier, but it simultaneously diminishes personal encounters that can enrich our lives. In essence, technology has perverted the grace of our gazing.

How do we embrace our *timor filialis*, our fear *for* goodness? Illich suggests, and we agree, that one way we can re-embody our senses is little practices of renunciation, of what I won't do—like writing letters on the computer—even though it is legitimate and functional. These little practices become a habit of practicing freedom from the world as it is. They are a way back to a person who stands apart from the constraints of the world, a person who lives from—in our words—a primary incentive for good, a person who lives from undistorted Desire, a person whose senses serve a spiritual function. They are little practices that sustain genuine encounters with others.

Illich is saying that we can damage our goodness either by the loss of connection with others or by the loss of connection with our sacred Desire. For our own goodness we need to stay aware of the subjectivity of the other and our self. By staying in connection, we protect our innate goodness.

Redemptive attuning seeks restoration based on engaging with others to redefine who and what they and we are. This is very different from feeling that we are the victim (as in a shame experience) who needs repair from another or that we are the perpetrator (as in a guilt experience) who needs correction or pardon. Rather, redemptive attuning requires the realization that our self is a participant within the subjective self of another and the other is a participant in our subjective self. Redemptive attuning leads to remorse when we realize that we together with the other participated in distorting the sacred Desire of each other. Remorse requires us to stay in mutual interactive communion until we both become aware of how we personally acted from our Second Nature and until we both take responsibility for having done so.

More specifically, redemptive attuning is the emotional and spiritual experience of knowing that our mirror neurons lead to our embodiment of the other and to the other's embodiment of us. This means that if we perpetrate hurt on another, we force the other to embody not only the hurt, but also our act of perpetration. Redemptive awareness, then, is seeing this dual evil: our sending out into the world—into another body—both the hurt and the act of perpetration. Alternatively, when we decline to hurt and we embody love, we are helping the other to embody love and to embody being one who loves. Our state of being becomes the state of being of another. This is the physiological equivalent of Thich Nhat Hahn's interbeing nature of people that we discussed in chapter 6.

The change wrought by redemptive attuning is more than the reparation of dissonance. It is more than a restoration to the innocent goodness of our infancy. It is the return to goodness, but now with the awareness gained through the experience of being redeemed from our Second Nature. We have the redemptive experience inside us. Having lived in redemptive attuning, we can carry this lived and living experience for others to embody. When the other will not or cannot stay in communion, we must seek those who can stay in loving communion with us so that we are redeemed. We can't be any other way but embodied in another.

This brings us to a psychobiological understanding of religious icons. In the Eastern Christian tradition an icon is a religious image of a face whose eyes serve as windows to God. Some contemporary contemplative prayer practices focus on silently looking into the eyes of a religious icon as a way of seeing and being seen by God.

Scientists who study mother-infant interactions refer to a Mother Icon. They have distinguished the infant's internalized neurobiological regulatory system that develops in relation to its mother from Bowlby's internalized working model of the mother and from internalized attachment patterns. They call the "pattern of 'experience-expectant' neurobiological development that is determined by the behavioral characteristics of the mother": the Mother Icon.[8] When the infant becomes self-regulating, it takes its Mother Icon with it into the environment where the internal Mother Icon regulates its relationships with others.

Whether we use religious icons, Illich's little practices of renunciation, or some other ritual, we can follow our sacred Desire into redemptive attuning. Earlier in this chapter, the story of the gang killer illustrates redemptive attuning at work between two human beings: mother with her son's killer. We can also journey into redemptive attuning by relating directly with the Divine. Such is the story of Albert Speer, who spent twenty years in Spandau Prison in Germany for war crimes and crimes against humanity that he rendered as Hitler's minister of armaments and war production.

Before turning to his story, we need to make two disclaimers. First, the actions of the Third Reich stand among the most evil of all time. To attempt redemption after participating in such massive evil is a great challenge. Some have recognized Albert Speer as someone who attempted to own his complicity and to accept such a challenge. No one can know the degree to which he personally succeeded. Second, we look at Albert Speer's story through the eyes of Miriam Pollard, a Cistercian nun of Mount St. Mary's Abbey in Wrentham, Massachusetts, who tells his story based on Speer's published memoir and diaries. She chose to study this man as an archetype of mercy. He clearly needed it. We choose Speer because he is such an extreme example of someone in his Second Nature acting from secondary incentives for good, which left him complicit with evil.

The frightening part of Speer's story, Pollard says, is that he was not a "bad man" in the usual sense of the word. He was simply ambitious, and his drive for glory committed him to Hitler and impelled him—because he didn't want to know—not to investigate what Hitler was doing.

SPIRITUAL CONSCIOUSNESS LEVELS AND POSSIBLE NEURAL CORRELATES

Ages	Spiritual Consciousness Level	Possible Neural Correlates
Birth–21	From archaic to rational consciousness (see Sidebar 1 for details)	Ordinary states of consciousness 1. Daily waking state We are aware of our perceptions, thoughts, and feelings. 2. Slow-wave sleep state Our awareness usually has no content. 3. Desynchronized sleep state We dream.
Some adults	Vision-logic consciousness	Meditative states of consciousness 1. Shallower 2. Deeper
	Psychic consciousness	Extraordinary alternative states 1. Heightened awareness 2. Absorption without sensate loss 3. Absorption with sensate loss Advanced extraordinary alternate states of consciousness
	Subtle consciousness	1. Insight-wisdom
	Christ consciousness	2. Ultimate being
	Nondual consciousness	3. Ongoing enlightened traits

As neurologist James Austin explains, the states of consciousness beyond the ordinary are accessed through religious and spiritual practices. Mystics of all great religions across cultures and

Sidebar continues

Spiritual Consciousness Levels
and Possible Neural Correlates, *continued*

time describe virtually identical experiences of the state of consciousness where their awareness senses unity and attuning with
all of creation and with the transcendent. Austin describes this
state as one of unbounded external and internal awareness and
considers it to be the advanced extraordinary alternate state of
consciousness characterized by ongoing enlightened traits.

Sources: James H. Austin, *Zen and the Brain* (Cambridge: MIT Press, 1999);
Jim Marion, *Putting on the Mind of Christ* (Charlottesville, Va.: Hampton Roads
Pub., 2000).

> For from that moment on, I was inescapably contaminated morally;
> from fear of discovering something which might have made me turn
> from my course, I had closed my eyes. This deliberate blindness out-
> weighs whatever good I may have done or tried to do in the face of
> it. Because I failed at that time, I still feel, to this day, responsible for
> Auschwitz in a wholly personal sense.[9]

In our sense of the word, Albert Speer was a bad man. That
is to say, he was a person locked in his Second Nature, operating
from secondary incentives for good. One secondary incentive for
good was ambition. He was ambitious for Hitler's and the public's
acclaim first as Hitler's favored architect and the designer of Nazi
spectaculars, then as minister of armaments and war production.
His ambition blinded him to what he was becoming a part of and
distorted his sacred Desire. As a result, he perpetrated evil.

But he woke up.

He began the journey of healing his distorted sacred Desire
when he became aware that he had blinded himself. He took the
next step in healing when he entered Spandau Prison. When

asked, "Albert Speer, why have you come?" Speer named his evil: "I have come to accept in myself the world's judgment on the Third Reich, to accept responsibility for my leadership. And to atone" (93). He accepted the acknowledgment of the world's judgment and repented by accepting responsibility for his participation. What did he do in prison? He took another step toward healing by choosing to atone. Then, he spent twenty years attempting to respond to grace, to being redeemed from the horror of what he came to see about himself.

> During the next twenty years of my life, I was guarded, in Spandau Prison, by nationals of the four powers against whom I had organized Hitler's war. Along with my six fellow-prisoners, they were the only people I had close contact with. Through them I learned directly what the effects of my work had been. Many of them mourned loved ones who had died in the war—in particular, every one of the Soviet guards had lost some close relative, brothers or a father. Yet not one of them bore a grudge toward me for my personal share in the tragedy; never did I hear words of recrimination. At the lowest ebb of my existence, in contact with these ordinary people, I encountered uncorrupted feelings of sympathy, helpfulness, human understanding, feeling that bypassed the prison rules. . . . And now, at last, I wanted to understand (73–74).

In the "uncorrupted feelings," Speer encountered redemptive attuning. Only grace could produce such kindness that transcended all human enmity. But Speer's moral stance alienated his fellow prisoners who did not choose to accept accountability. His diaries reveal that at the best of times these men lacked relational skills. At the worst of times, pettiness marked the community.

For his transformation Speer needed more than the attuning he could glean from those around him. He established for himself a kind of monastic existence where his relationship with God redeemed him. He lived largely in silence and relative poverty. He didn't even have a name; he was "Number Five." He committed himself to a plan, which was to build a garden, and he lived in daily obedience to his plan. He tended his linden trees, hauled bricks for terracing, planted beds of iris beside carefully planned walks, and made an old bathtub into a pool. He lived the journey of redemptive attuning. His garden was the visible expression of his self in the process of redemption. It was beautiful to him as a projection of his hope for redemption.

Speer went to church and sometimes he was the only man to meet with Chaplain Casalis. He listened to Casalis's words about God and read books that the chaplain gave him. He read widely. From his readings, he added to his spiritual practice. Speer seemed to give himself what the influential twentieth-century theologian Hans Urs von Balthasar describes as "Unconditional priority . . . to the placing of oneself [himself] entirely at the disposal of divine love . . . to the superiority of a life given purely as an answer to God's [the Divine's] self-giving love."[10] As he gave himself to grace, Speer got a new idea.

> I have a new idea to make myself exercise to the point of exhaustion: I have begun, along with the garden work, to walk the distance from Berlin to Heidelberg—626 kilometers! For that purpose I have marked out a circular course in the garden. . . . If I had taken a different route, along the prison wall, I could have made my track 350 meters. But because of the better view, I prefer this other track. This project is a training of the will, a battle against the endless boredom; but it is also an expression of the last remnants of my urge toward status and activity.[11]

In walking, Speer was doing many things. As he acknowledges, he was wearing out his secondary incentive for good, his urge toward status. He endured boredom and, perhaps, in that boredom saw more of his secondary incentives for good. In addition, by imagining real people and real places, he was practicing resonant attuning. He valued what he imagined rather than treating the people and places as objects for his manipulation. He was

walking not to get acclaim or to reduce his prison sentence; he was
walking to build relationships to life. He puts it thus:

> On the stretch from Salzburg to Vienna, I several times had to fight
> boredom; several times I was on the point of quitting the whole thing.
> Merely covering distance no longer satisfies me; it's too abstract
> just to count the kilometers. I must make it all more vivid. Perhaps
> I should take the idea of hiking around the world quite literally and
> conceive each segment in full detail. For that purpose I would have to
> obtain maps and books and familiarize myself fully with the segment
> immediately ahead; the landscape, the climate, the people and their
> culture, their occupations, their manner of life (147).

By the time he was released from Spandau Prison, he had, fig-
uratively speaking, walked around the world and, in so doing, he
came to value the world. He also wrote his memoirs and his diaries as a warning to the world and as a confession to his family.
This gave him the strength to survive depression and the prison's
devaluation of his personal worth. For those he loved (his wife
and his daughter), he hid his anguish when they visited him and
he prayed for them at other times. He also developed the custom
of praying for any unknown persons who had heard of him and
prayed for him.

Perhaps the one human relationship that most unconditionally
sustained Speer in redemptive attuning was his relationship with
Annemarie Kempf, his secretary. Speer was her life. During and
after Spandau, she carried along with him his inconsolable pain.
She also worked with disabled children until her death, and Speer
assisted her work financially from his publishing royalties.

Asks Miriam Pollard, "was the Speer of the Nuremberg Trial
the same man who left Spandau in the storm of flashbulbs on Sep-
tember 30, 1966?" "Hardly," she answers.

> Forgiveness is a complex business. As he enters the gates of Span-
> dau, he is carrying his objective innocence in a personality still

wounded and confused by early emotional deprivation and the destructive choices of his life. He has a long way to go, but not alone. Spandau had a purpose, to Speer himself and to the world. In giving himself to the work of personal reconstruction, he was carrying a wounded world into the heart of God [the Divine]. In giving his own moral wounds to be healed, wounds acquired through embracing the destructive values of his world, he was helping to cleanse that world . . . of the damage wrought by those values. Conversion [redemption] works this way for all of us. It is not a work of isolation. In our personal remaking our world comes with us. . . . His was the terrible vocation of recognizing the evil into which he had allowed himself to be drawn. . . . In silence and solitude, poverty and stability, his own transformation was helping to transform the world (33–34).

Redemptive attuning is stepping out of the mechanics of nature into the mystery of nature. Speer was doing the work of sustaining mystery rather than the work of sustaining mastery.

"Spandau was not the harshest part of Albert Speer's life: its sequel was. . . . He was damned by those who condemned as disloyalty his last minute repudiation of Hitler and damned by those who could never accept him into the 'other side'" (171, 174). While in prison, Speer did not redeem the entire world. Second Nature still lived in many of those around him as the following story shows.

A Jewish woman, survivor of the death camps, who had married a German government official, found herself at a reception for Albert Speer. She said to him with remarkable courtesy, "Herr Speer, please forgive me. I hope you will understand that I cannot remain here." He replied quietly, "It is I who need your forgiveness, and I understand more than you think I do" (173).

Speer's response reflects his state of redemption. He did not engage with the distortion of his Desire that the dissonant attuning of the woman could have caused. He did not retaliate and thereby contribute further to the destruction he had helped perpetuate. Instead, he asked for forgiveness. Through it all "God [the Divine] was lover and destiny for Speer. He [God/the Divine] would not let him settle for less" (32).

Nor will the Divine let us settle for less. As von Balthasar tells us, "Love . . . means unconditional commitment, which . . . includes a willingness to go all the way to one's death."[12] In our terminology this means going all the way to the death of our Second Nature. This does not return us to our original First Nature. It brings us to a new creation of our First Nature, where we know good and evil. Second Nature redeemed contributes to the world a richness and depth that otherwise wouldn't have been.

Redemptive attuning requires redeeming our memories. Miroslav Volf, professor of systematic theology at Yale Divinity School, tells us that redeeming memories involves three tasks. First, we must remember truthfully. Second, we must remember therapeutically. In our words, "remembering therapeutically" means changing our memories formed in dissonant attuning experiences into memories formed in resonant attuning. We can do this, according to Volf, either by giving the dissonant memories a positive meaning or by labeling them as a sense-less segment of our past. Finally, we must learn from our past. We must remember rightly. "Remembering rightly" refers to what is right for the person who has been attuned to with dissonance, what is right for those who have attuned dissonantly, and what is right for the larger community.[13] We would add to Professor Volf's three tasks that memories are not only psychological phenomena, they are also physiological and biological phenomena. When we redeem our memories, we modify both the psychological and the physiological/biological aspects of them.

As we cycle and recycle through the process of healing our distorted Desire, redeeming our memories, and redeeming our Second Nature, we come more fully to know that we have divinity within us. This frees us to act accordingly. In the words of Ralph Waldo Emerson, "He who does a good deed is instantly ennobled. He who does a mean deed is by the action itself contracted. He who puts off impurity, thereby puts on purity. If a man is at heart just, then in so far is he God."[14]

When we act from the divinity within us, redemptive attuning opens sacred Desire into community. In our next chapter we will look more extensively at the restorative work of and within community.

CHAPTER 9

INCARNATED SPIRIT

The Work of Restoring Community

> We are caught in an inescapable network of mutuality, tied in a single garment of destiny. Whatever affects one directly, affects all indirectly.
>
> —MARTIN LUTHER KING JR.

ONCE WE EXPERIENCE redemptive attuning and can live more in our redeemed First Nature, the sacred Desire embodied within us is freer to be translated through us into community. Sacred Desire urges us to take our redeemed First Nature spirit into our relationships so that other people can incarnate it. The work of restoring community is to find ways of being together where this can happen—where our redeemed First Nature spirit can become incarnated in each and every person in our community.

Community is inherent in human life. In our most basic biology, we are social beings. We are interconnected with one another —through our attuning—whether we want it or not and whether we recognize it or not. Our communities can be either healthy or unhealthy.

Healthy communities support people who relate from redeemed First Nature. These people, who have been transformed into redemptive awareness, can recognize and own their Second Nature when they live in it. Because they see that sending their wounds into community perpetrates their wounds in others, they choose not to do so. Instead they heal their wounds, repair their Second Nature, and restore themselves to First Nature.

Unhealthy communities foster divisions that reflect the inner split of people living in unrecognized Second Nature. These unrecognized and unrepaired divisions become warring factions within community. To repeat the words of Martin Luther King Jr., "Whatever affects one directly, affects all indirectly."[1]

The work of restoring community is bidirectional. The more we live in our redeemed First Nature within our community, the more we restore community in the direction of health. The healthier the community, the more it restores and supports people living in their redeemed First Nature.

All of us individually live in both our First Nature and our Second Nature. All of our communities contain a combination of people living in First Nature and people living in Second Nature. Our challenge is to create communities that will foster an increasing number of people who live most of the time in redeemed First Nature. Science and religion are showing us how to do this work of restoring community.

His Holiness the Dalai Lama is a person who recognizes that both science and religion are affirming our interconnectedness and our primary invisible reality (our incarnated spirit). Moreover, he supports a productive dialogue between scientists and people of faith. His words echo those of Martin Luther King Jr.'s epigraph above. The Dalai Lama calls for a moral outlook "that recognizes the fundamental interconnected nature of all living beings and their environment."[2]

Born into a family of simple farmers, His Holiness was enthroned—at the age of six—as the Fourteenth Dalai Lama in the Tibetan capital of Lhasa. He complemented his education in Buddhism with a hobby of dismantling and reassembling mechanical objects such as a pocket watch and two hand-cranked film projectors. His fascination with technology led to his fascination with science.

Forced to flee Tibet in 1959, he took up residence in Dharamsala, India, where he has headed the Tibetan government-in-exile. During his international travels, he has met and become friends with distinguished scientists such as physicist David Bohm. His interest in science culminated in 1987 with the first Mind and Life Conference—a weeklong conference held every two years—where scientists, the Dalai Lama, and philosophers of science engage in private discussions. After decades of study, the Dalai Lama has come to respect both science and spirituality as complementing each other in their views of truth.

We carry forward his respect as we approach understanding that which exists beyond our subjective imagination—that which is "real" even though we cannot see it or scientifically measure it. Spiritual traditions have long described this reality. It has been revealed in Asia, in Hinduism and Buddhism, in Taoism, Confucianism, and Shintoism. The Hindu tradition, for example, describes *saccidananda*, which we are told means absolute Being (*sat*) in pure consciousness (*cit*) of perfect bliss or joy (*ananda*). The Buddhist tradition speaks of *dharmakaya*, which is said to be the experience of nondual consciousness, and *nirvana*, which is the realization of oneness of self with the nondual absolute reality that is the ground of being and the cessation of suffering.

The Muslim tradition holds that Muhammad was God's messenger. He transmitted the divine revelation, which is the Quran—the literal word of God. He is also honored and respected as a living moral model of the Quran's teachings in both private and public life.

The Christian tradition teaches that God is revealed in the man Jesus. The Dominican philosopher and spiritual master Meister Eckhart explains, "the Word, the Son in the Godhead" is 'what-it-is' . . . the definition itself . . . reveals the 'what' of the subject and the 'why' of its qualities."[3] And the great Benedictine religious leader of the twentieth century, Bede Griffiths, is quoted as saying:

> Wherever man wakes to consciousness and knows himself in his basic intuitive consciousness as open to the transcendent mystery of existence, the power of the Spirit is in him, drawing him to eternal life. The presence of the Spirit in this sense can be traced in all the religions of mankind.[4]

The intuitive wisdom of indigenous people (the Australian Aborigines, the Polynesian Islanders, the African Bushmen, the Native American Indians, and the Eskimos) has told of the quality that exists beyond logic and reason. The Navajo philosophy speaks of *hozro,* the balance of human beings with world and spirit.

Throughout this book we have been showing how *biological* and *psychological* sciences are confirming what spiritual wisdom has long known. *Physical* science also lends its support. For example, the friend of the Dalai Lama, professor of theoretical physics David Bohm, is best known for his theory of the implicate/explicate order. What spiritual traditions describe as nondual primary reality, Bohm calls the implicate order. The implicate order is the invisible energy of all life that is present behind the explicate order of the world as we know it. The visible explicate order is the product of the invisible reality. The invisible reality is what endures and continually unfolds in visible forms.

Quantum physics carries this theory forward by acknowledging that all matter consists of fields of energy. These fields of energy are structured to form what we see in daily life, for example, our human body, plants, animals, and all matter. Furthermore, quantum physics shows us that matter, together with time and space, exist in relationship to the level of awareness with which we perceive all three. The twenty-first century faces the mystery of putting what we know into the perspective of a larger dynamic energy system.

The bottom line is that the ultimate reality to which we are attuning is not a projection of our imagination. It is a reality that has been known through the ages by various names, *saccidananda, dharmakaya,* God, *hozro,* implicate order, and fields of energy. Each name reflects the perspective of the people describing it. But what they are describing is ultimate reality, which is a nondual eternal state of being.

This means that the Divine is not just whatever any one person perceives. Although many paths show us some portion of the Divine, there is only one ultimate reality. All perspectives contribute to our intuiting ultimate reality. The work of restoring community is to find ways of being together where—living in First Nature nondualistic awareness—we value all our different perspectives and incarnate each other's spirit rather than, living in Second Nature dualistic awareness, we fight about which perspective is the right perspective.

From the findings of neuroscience and psychology, we know that we are created with the potential for doing this. From birth, we are neurologically equipped to read and respond to subtle expressions on the faces of caregivers (such as smiles, frowns, or grimaces) and to hear and respond to subtle tones of the human voice. This processing of information from the environment—called our social engagement system—takes place in our brain without our conscious awareness (see "Neuroception," page 24).[5] Our social engagement system is linked into our physiology through our autonomic nervous system.

Specifically, the muscles of our face and head that have evolutionarily originated along with our autonomic nervous system equip us biologically to regulate each other through the social engagement system (see "The Polyvagal System," page 27). The regulation is bidirectional. We regulate ourselves and we regulate each other in community and vice versa. When we live in a physiology of calm, safety, and valuing, our social engagement system helps us pass that on to the people in our community. Likewise, when we live in a physiology of fear, we pass that to those in our community.

Furthermore, we have mirror neurons that automatically activate brain circuits when we carry out actions, express emotions, and experience sensations. Our mirror neurons also activate when we observe in others these actions, emotions, and sensations (see "Gazing," page 14). This shared activation suggests a mechanism of "embodied simulation."[6] Embodied simulation is how we take into our bodies and experientially live what we see. Through our mirror neurons we incarnate our own spirit and the spirit of others. And we take our own spirit into the world to be incarnated by others.

More literally, perhaps, than Martin Luther King Jr. knew at the time that he spoke: "We are caught in an inescapable network of mutuality, tied in a single garment of destiny." Realizing our interconnectedness (spiritually, psychologically, and biologically) calls us to take responsibility for how our sacred Desire moves us out into community. Because we know that we are brain-wired to perceive and respond to others, we know that our First Nature is susceptible to dysregulation when we are in the company of people who are strangers or who are in their Second Nature. Automatically, dysregulation propels us into our Second Nature. We slide into left-brain hemisphere, power and control, power potion–mediated (see "Imagine Your Brain," page 16), self-preservative behavior.[7] Living in our Second Nature with our Desire distorted by secondary incentives for good, we take into the world behavior that distorts the Desire of all those we touch. Our garment of destiny becomes one of mutual destruction as we act in self-protective ways.

What the work of restoring community requires, however, is that we bring our redeemed First Nature into our relationships. Then we bring to life our right-brain hemisphere, secure attachment behavior, reverence and synchrony, holy nectar mediated (see "The Holy Nectar," page 5), and species-preservative behavior.[8] The feelings associated with species-preservative behavior include "attachment, love, empathy, compassion, trust, reverence and joy."[9] In our redeemed First Nature we can own and take responsibility for what we see about ourselves through redemptive awareness. Living in our redeemed First Nature, where our Desire expresses a primary incentive for good, we take into the world species-protective behavior. We weave a garment of destiny that restores our communities to mutual compassion.

This is not easy to do. We are always affected by one another's Second Nature. Hypervigilance and its opposite, emotional numbing, are aspects of our Second Nature. When we live in these aspects, we bring them into community. "Emotional withdrawal, emotional numbing and denial can anesthetize our sense of compassion, empathy and humanity. In this state, violence can be inflicted upon others without remorse or conflict."[10] We lose our capacity for secure attachment and create communities based in self-protection. When we do so, we create communities where people fight among themselves and where they go to war with other communities.

But we do not need to remain stuck in our Second Nature. We can wake up, heal, and be redeemed. Then in our redeemed First Nature, we can create communities where we experience safety and where our species-protective behaviors can emerge. These are communities characterized by a predominance of people with an awareness of ultimate reality, by a growing number of people with a tolerance for different perspectives about ultimate reality, by people willing to enter into dialogue where they listen to each other until they can trust each other, and by people attempting to relate from redeemed First Nature as they seek to repair the effects they perpetrate on others when they fail to relate from redeemed First Nature. Such communities foster redemptive attuning, which encourages more and more people to gain greater access to their redeemed First Nature.

We would go so far as to say that the incarnated spirit's work of restoring community is to create among us a community identity. Our community identity reflects our innate interrelatedness, our mutuality where the basic interests of others serve the essential interests of our self. Our community identity integrates our individual distinctions and encourages us to live freely from our sacred Desire to be in resonant and redemptive attuning with one another. Living freely from our sacred Desire to be in resonant and redemptive attuning with one another would then satisfy both our community identity and also shape "our single garment of destiny." The more people enter community in redemptive states, the more we can direct our human destiny toward living in and out of our sacred Desire as an expression of our divinity.

Actually, whether we are aware of it or not, we live always in a community identity of mutuality. When we neglect this, we become oblivious to the reality that we are made *by* love to live *in* and *for* love. This obliviousness permits dishonesty and abuse of others that literally damages the living tissue in our human brains and corrupts the communities that constitute our identities. Out of touch with our sacred Desire, we are no longer free to receive life with a spirit of gratitude.

What will it take to wake us up to our community identity? What will it take to change the living tissue of our brains so that we live more completely *from* our redeemed First Nature sacred Desire and *for* our species-protective community identity? What will it take for us to wake up and see the Divine—the incarnated Spirit—in everyone?

In an editorial, The Most Reverend Rowan Williams, Archbishop of Canterbury, describes what it took to awaken one young man.

> A few weeks ago, I took part in a discussion that involved a number
> of people working with children and young people who suffer from

different forms of autism—the kind of disorder that seems to cut people off from ordinary communication and shows itself in strange repetitive behaviors and sometimes in violent outbursts. We watched a video showing the work of one of the most experienced therapists in Britain, and then heard her talking about what she is trying to do with her methods.

The first thing we saw on the video was a young man, severely disturbed, beating his head against a wall, and then walking fast up and down the room, twisting and flicking a piece of string. The therapist's first response was strange: She began to twist and flick a piece of string as well. When the young man made a noise, so did she; when he began to do something different, like banging his hand on a table, she did the same.

The video showed what happened over two days. By the end of the two days, the boy had begun to smile at her and to respond when touched. A relation had been created. And what the therapist said about it was this: Autism arises when the brain senses too much material coming in, too much information. There is a feeling of panic; the mind has to regain control. And the best way of doing this is to close up on yourself and repeat actions that are familiar; do nothing new, and don't acknowledge anything coming from outside. But when the therapist gently echoes the actions and rhythms, the anxious and wounded mind of the autistic person sees that there is after all a link with the outside world that isn't threatening.

Here is someone doing what I do; the world isn't just an unfamiliar place of terror and uncertainty. And when I do this, I can draw out an answer, and echo; I'm not powerless. And so relationship begins.[11]

Archbishop Williams is describing how the mirror neurons of the autistic boy may link him with the actions and rhythms of the therapist. Together they co-created a we-centric space, a space where—in their mutual attuning—each knew he was known by the other. In the we-centric space, the boy's experience of embodied simulation gave him a sense of familiarity that he and the therapist were alike. This invited him to participate in a mutual Desire to abide in love. He could acknowledge the therapist with a smile and allow the resonant attuning of their mirror neurons to heal him.[12]

THE CIRCLE OF SECURITY PROJECT

"The Circle of Security Project is a 20-week, group-based, parent education and psychotherapy intervention designed to shift patterns of attachment-caregiving interactions in high-risk caregiver-child dyads to a more appropriate developmental pathway. All phases of the [project], including the pre- and post-intervention assessments, and the intervention itself, are based on attachment theory and procedures, current research on early relationships, and object relations theory. Using . . . videotapes of their interactions with their children, caregivers are encouraged:

1. to increase their sensitivity and appropriate responsiveness to the child's signals [to move away from the caregiver in order to explore, and the child's signals to move back to the caregiver] for comfort and soothing;

2. to increase their ability to reflect on their own and the child's behavior, thoughts and feelings regarding their attachment-caregiving interactions; and

3. to reflect on experiences in their own histories that affect their current caregiving patterns."

Source: Robert Marvin, Glen Cooper, Kent Hoffman and Bert Powell, "The Circle of Security Project: Attachment-based Intervention with Caregiver-Pre-school Child Dyads," *Attachment and Human Development* 4, no. 1 (2002): 107.

Here we should pause to distinguish between two actions: being healed and being cured. Probably the boy in this video was not cured, and yet he was clearly being healed so that he could relinquish his destructive behavior, which was his coping mechanism, his secondary incentive for good. He could relinquish beating his head against a wall. Instead, he could allow smiling and touching. Others we know have been cured of some illness, but have not been healed of their fear of recurrence or redeemed from their bitterness about the suffering they've endured. To be healed is to be set free from fear and all its secondary incentives for good that cause us pain. To be redeemed is to be transformed to live a life of communion and sharing in love.

Whatever affects us affects all others because we are made so that we can respond to each other in a resonant attuning way that moves us all toward wholeness. Von Balthasar—speaking theologically—puts it thus: "The people who live entirely for love . . . are . . . our intercessors and chosen helpers. . . . [T]heir lives and deeds open up to one another and mutually interpenetrate. . . . [T]here is always a responsibility . . . to enter every situation as a representative of the whole and of the comprehensive idea of love."[13]

Finding ways to create we-centric spaces of love—wombs of compassion—restores us and those whom our lives touch to wholeness. In we-centric spaces of love, "we do not just love the other for who the other is; we love because we know that we are part of the other and the other is part of us. This is love that recognizes connectedness at the deepest level."[14] This is the incarnated spirit moving us from self-protective to species-protective behavior.

All cultures have traditions and rituals that provide ways to create wombs of compassion where we can meet safely to share our needs. The sidebars in this chapter provide other examples of attempts to create safe places. In the following letter to Abby, Rabbi Craig H. Ezring describes a personal example of creating a we-centric space.

DEAR ABBY: After reading the letters about hospital gowns, I thought I'd share my story. I am a rabbi. When I first trained as a chaplain, I was taught to make my hospital rounds in full dress—wearing a suit and tie, with my jacket buttoned. However, one

Camp Barnabas

Camp Barnabas is a nondenominational Christian camp that exists to offer childhood experiences to kids with life-threatening illness or disability. Located on 123 acres of natural beauty, all facilities are wheelchair-accessible.

"WaterWorks" is complete with waterslides, fountains, a wheelchair beach entry, and cabanas. Tucked below the awe-inspiring view from the bluff is a hidden creek where campers fish, launch canoes, and welcome boisterous kids back from their innertubing expeditions.

High-adventure activities include rappelling off the bluff at "Inspiration Point" and a complete ropes course strung among the treetops thirty feet above the ground. Horseback riding, archery, and the rifle range offer additional activities for outdoor entertainment. Of course, no camp would be complete without an arts and crafts program, drama, and music. There are always new baby animals for the petting zoo and other low-adventure activities for those so inclined.

The fun doesn't stop when the sun goes down. Every evening is capped off with a themed party that is creative and energetic.

Counselor-to-camper ratios are 1:1 for campers with special needs and 1:3 for siblings without disabilities. Doctors and nurses staff the medical clinic 24/7.

Campers should be at least seven years of age. Summer sessions last seven days. Limited sponsorships are available to help offset financial burden.

Source: Camp Barnabas Web site, www.campbarnabas.org.

day a patient expressed that although she needed to talk to me, she felt terribly uncomfortable lying there "in a hospital gown with her tuchas sticking out" while I sat there in a three-piece suit.

I stood up, told her I'd be back in a moment, went to the nurse's station and got a hospital gown. I took off my suit, donned the gown over my briefs and T-shirt, and headed straight back to the patient's room. The minute she saw me in that gown, she brightened and relaxed enough to open up about all the concerns on her mind.

The visit took a little longer than usual, and when I finished our session with a prayer for healing, I rose from the chair. As I did, the sound as my thighs ripping themselves from the Naugahyde brought a huge smile to both our faces. I was laughing so hard I forgot to hold the back of the gown as I headed back down the hall—so I was exposed.

I learned an important lesson on creativity that day. But I also learned that two hospital gowns are better than one—if you remember to put one on backward.[15]

Rabbi Ezring wanted to hold the patient in resonant attuning by experiencing her as if she were inside him. To do so, he literally put himself into her dilemma so that he lived her experience and he let her see him in it. In other words, he experienced her exposure and let "his tuchas stick out."

We all have nervous systems that are capable of doing what he did. He created a relationship in which that hospital encounter became the reason for his being in harmony with the patient's need for mutuality. In mutuality, they co-created a we-centric space that allowed the patient to resonate with him and he with her. The we-centric space—a womb of compassion—became the means of the woman's healing. Such acts are the incarnated Spirit at work in us restoring our communities to wholeness. We human beings have the capacity to bring goodness into the world when we Desire to communicate joy.

We authors experienced an astounding encounter with such an enfleshment of the Divine. Her name was Sarah Johnson, and we both met her—on different occasions—at St. Benedict's Monastery in Snowmass, Colorado. She seemed an unlikely incarnation of the holy. From the age of eleven months when Sarah fell and damaged the back of her brain, which left her paralyzed, she could do nothing for herself. But from the time of the accident, her parents kept her in places where she could meet others.

InnerKids

Founded in 2001, InnerKids is a national leader in teaching mindful awareness to children in pre-K through middle school. Mindful awareness is a state of present attention in which one observes thoughts, feelings, emotions, and events at the moment they occur without reacting to them in an automatic or habitual way. InnerKids' mindful awareness activities take into account children's developmental differences, train focused attention and awareness, and acknowledge clarity and compassion as part of the process of becoming more attentive and aware. As world events become increasingly complicated, it is critical that children learn to view them from a nuanced perspective—something that can arise only from a calm and focused mind.

Sources: Daniel J. Siegel, *The Mindful Brain: Reflection and Attunement in the Cultivation of Well-being* (New York: W. W. Norton, 2007), 330–31.

www.InnerKids.org

We met her when she was twenty-seven years old. Sarah lay helplessly on a mat that was placed upon a kitchen counter of the retreat house where her mother, Pat, worked as a cook. The counter lifted her up to our waist level. She could see us and be seen. Unable to speak, Sarah sometimes would give an ecstatic whoop as though something struck her as funny. She had great fun! And she never rejected anyone.

Her eyes welcomed each of us in the only way she could. When gazing into her eyes, both of us authors felt like we were looking into the eyes of God. Open to everyone, she perfectly embodied the essence of God in her gaze of love.

Thomas Keating, a Cistercian priest who resides at the monastery, has said, "She is probably the only person I've ever met who had no false self. She injured her brain at the very time that the false self begins to form. So God was able to have someone in the world who remained completely childlike all her life."[16]

In our terminology, Sarah remained in her original First Nature. She lived her thirty-four years in First Nature. During that time—without any effort—she rose to ever increasing admiration and power among the monks and visitors. A complete paralytic, she became the star of a sophisticated retreat house.[17]

Through total surrender Sarah manifested the incarnated spirit. We, who were blessed to know her, learned much about our being through our moments of meeting with the Divine in her gaze. In those moments we experienced redemptive attuning where our sacred Desire changed our being through an encounter with love.

This is the work of restoring community. We become who we are by being seen, and when we are seen with love, we become love. We become whole; we become holy. Then, we can realize, as philosopher Teilhard de Chardin reputedly has said, "We are not human beings having a spiritual experience, but spiritual beings having a human experience."

When a critical mass of people live in redeemed First Nature spirit, then we can transform the world. We transform the world —not by coercion—but by being incarnated spirits for others to embody, as we will see in the next chapter.

CHAPTER 10

TOWARD A WORLD OF COMPASSION

Beginning to Live and Love Globally

> [H]ave no fear of human sin. Love [people] even in [their] sin, for that is the semblance of Divine Love and is the highest love on earth. Love all of God's creation, the whole and every grain of sand of it. Love every leaf, every ray of God's light. Love the animals, love the plants, love everything. If you love every thing, you will perceive the divine mystery in things. Once you perceive it, you will begin to comprehend it better every day. And you will come at last to love the whole world with an all-embracing love.
>
> —FYODOR DOSTOYEVSKY, *The Brothers Karamazov*

SACRED DESIRE is not simply an avenue for healing and a source of personal hope that touches us and those with whom we most closely live and work each day. We ardently believe that it also charts a path toward developing and nourishing a world of compassion. Compassion is

"kind, receptive openness," "an attitude of lowliness," "a meekness that does not defend itself," "long-suffering patience," and thus the winning over, the enduring of one's unendurable brothers [and sisters].[1]

It is perceiving, in Dostoyevsky's words, "the divine mystery in things."[2] Compassion is perceiving "the world *as* gift; *as* radically dependent on God [the Divine]; as not just often productive of evil but *as* something ambiguous, at once good and profoundly distorted; *as* promised, an eschatological consummation by God [the Divine]; and *as* redeemed."[3]

Thus far we have seen how sacred Desire helps us overcome our individually learned distortions and heals us. We have seen how sacred Desire leads us into redemptive attuning, which transforms us into a redeemed First Nature. And we have seen how sacred Desire moves us to take our redeemed First Nature spirit into community where it can be incarnated. Now we will look at how sacred Desire poises us to build up a critical mass of people who are living in redeemed First Nature with an incarnated spirit. This critical mass of people—using their right-brain hemisphere, their secure attachments, their reverence and synchrony with the life force of the universe, and their holy nectar–mediated species-preservative behavior—offer the promise of finding ways to live and love globally. They carry the potential for solving the monumental problems of our world: war, declining economy, chronic health care crisis, and potentially devastating climate change.

These are people who freely express their sacred Desire. They can see the needs of the wider world in which we live through the eyes of interrelatedness. They can "see the world in truth as an event of abounding communion . . . as being for joy and one receives and gives the divine joy that pulses as the heart of it."[4] These are people who, with joy, can begin to co-create we-centric spaces of love where reparative justice can prevail in the fair distribution of resources. These are people who can begin to move us toward a world of compassion.

As Jon Kabat-Zinn, PhD, founding director of the Center for
Mindfulness in Medicine, Health Care, and Society at the University of Massachusetts Medical School, puts it:

> The world needs all its flowers, just as they are, and even though they
> bloom for only the briefest moments, which we call a lifetime. It is
> our job to find out one by one and collectively what kind of flowers
> we are, and to share our unique beauty with the world in the precious
> time that we have, and to leave the children and grandchildren a leg-
> acy of wisdom and compassion embodied in the way we live, in our
> institutions, and in our honoring our interconnectedness, at home
> and around the world.[5]

Conversely, a failure to honor interconnectedness in any one
relationship is a failure of world community, a failure of compassion. We see such failures daily. A dramatic example occurred
in May 2006 when several parties were climbing Mount Ever-
est. While descending—after completing his climb to the sum-
mit—David Sharp collapsed from oxygen deficiency and lay dying.
Other climbers passed him by to continue their climb. In a world
of compassion, this would not have happened. Despite anger at
Sharp for interrupting their climb, despite disappointment at not
finishing what they had prepared and gone for, climbers would
have stopped to help Sharp out. In the words of von Balthasar,
"Within the cosmic order, the only foundation for love is the natural harmony of all the parts of the cosmos; the only foundation is
being, working, experiencing, and suffering with one another . . . ,
being pervaded by a single, common, cosmic breath."[6]

Being pervaded by a single, common, cosmic breath is living in
a body of love—of oxytocin triggering oxytocin—where our flesh is
alive, vital, and connected to all other flesh by mirror neurons that
mediate interpersonal resonant and redemptive attuning. Professor of psychology Louis Cozolino confirms what we have been saying throughout this book when he tells us that human beings have

evolved as social creatures with interwoven brains. Our brains, he says, are social organs built through interpersonal experience. Relationships have the power to reshape our brains throughout life.[7] Relationships have the power to open us to the love that created everything. Being in harmony with the love of creation, however, includes an element of unpredictability.

That unpredictability expresses itself in our freedom—not to do anything we want but—to live free from fear, to Desire good and to be good. Freedom from fear opens us to novelty, to the adventure of each and every person being valued and offered the opportunity and encouragement to express the one person he or she most deeply is. It opens us to communal participation in discovering how to foster mutual Desire to abide in love and in nourishing the unitive power of sacred Desire that can overcome the violence in our world. This is vitally important in the twenty-first century where—because advancing technology has shrunk the dimensions of the globe—we live together around the world more closely and more immediately than ever before.

When, then, can we learn to love globally and live in a world of compassion? There are two general answers to this question—answers that have been posed by others but that we will address from our perspective. First, we learn when we must. Second, we learn when we see role models of those who successfully love globally.

We learn when we must. This is the old answer: Necessity is the mother of invention. Never has it been truer than in today's world of rapid communication and escalating violence—to ourselves and to our environment—which demands that we *must* learn to love globally. Fortunately, there seem to be biological, sociocultural, economic, and political forces in the world today with the potential for moving us to live more completely from our sacred Desire.

The biological and sociocultural forces are described by Christopher Boehm, the cultural anthropologist who has been most influential in developing the concept of egalitarianism as the

CONTINUUM OF SOCIAL GROUP FUNCTIONING

Science is lending understanding about how social-group functioning persists over time and gives rise to the groups' worldview. We know that people process, store, retrieve, and respond to the world in a state-dependent fashion.

In a state of calm, a person's neocortex can appreciate complexity and process information in ways that are future focused and creative. In a state of anxiety, a person's amygdala in the midbrain is activated, and information processing becomes concrete and superstitious. In a state of terror, major shifts in brain-stem/autonomic nervous system predominate, and information processing is focused on and reactionary to the present. These states, over time, become the traits that characterize our person.

Social-Environmental Pressures

	Stable/Safe Environment	Unpredictable Environment	Threatening Environment
Cognitive style	Abstract Creative	Concrete Superstitious	Reactive Regressive
Affective "tone"	Calm	Anxiety	Terror
System solution	Innovative	Simplistic	Reactionary
Time focus of solution	Future	Immediate Future	Present
Rules, regulations, and laws	Abstract Conceptual	Intrusive Superstitious	Reactive Punitive
Child-rearing practices	Nurturing Flexible Encircling	Ambivalent Obsessive Controlling	Apathetic Oppressive Harsh
Worldview	*Unity*[a]	*Good or evil*	*Evil*

[a]"Unity" is *absolutely* beyond description; it is neither good nor evil.

Over time our states change us on a molecular, structural, and functional level. As we transform our worldview of a split between good or evil to one of unity, our physiology changes from one of fear to one of love. Our autonomic nervous system shifts from sympathetic (fight/flight) or dorsal vagal (freeze) reactions to ventral vagal regulation of social cuing. This allows our brains, literally, to grow new brain cells and make new neural connections as we re-member our brains into more complex integration and ourselves into evolving integrity-of-wholeness.

The persistence and influence of social group functioning over time carries implications for child-rearing. Given the amount of physical and emotional violence in American homes that children are exposed to, given the increasing violence on television, in videogames, music, and films that children see and hear, given community and school violence that confronts children, how can we possibly nurture a worldview of good? Obviously, the first step is to reduce children's exposure to unpredictable and threatening environments and to increase children's exposure to stable and safe environments. We also need to increase our face-to-face human interactions between individuals of all age groups. We learn our being by encounter. When our children watch television, they are not seeing and being seen by our human face of the Divine. We need our children and our world to be formed by our embodied divine presence.

Source: Adapted from Bruce D. Perry, MD, PhD, "The Neurodevelopmental Impact of Violence in Childhood," in *Textbook of Child and Adolescent Forensic Psychiatry*, ed. D. Schetky and E. Benedek (Washington, D.C.: American Psychiatric Press, 2001), 221–38.

starting point for studying all modern institutions. He defines *egalitarianism* as that product of human intentionality where people "consciously create, and carefully enforce, egalitarian plans" to keep tendencies to hierarchy decisively reversed. Boehm presents persuasive ethnographic evidence to support his hypothesis that the evolution of human beings has resulted in the biological selection of genes for altruism. He concludes that the evolutionary saga has brought us to the point where we are "a species altruistic enough to cooperate quite efficiently in large or small groups, but at the same time prone to competition and conflict."[8] Our challenge is to maximize our altruism, which is based in love, and to minimize our selfishness, which is based in fear.

Egalitarianism requires active effort to keep the will to power undermined. Subordinates must unite—as did our forefathers who revolted against the English sovereign—to reduce inequality. The whole group must select leaders carefully. Only those who value equality should be permitted to guide us.

In addition to Boehm's biological and sociocultural influences, economic forces also seem to be steering us toward compassionate living. Thomas Friedman, the Pulitzer Prize–winning foreign affairs columnist at the *New York Times*, explains how globalization flattened the world at the dawn of the twenty-first century.[9] His idea is that economic globalization makes war more difficult because a warring nation risks being left out of the insourcing and outsourcing loop. Globalization thus can encourage compliance with and greater understanding of each other. Though Friedman's intent is not to promote compassion, we authors believe that his conceptualization of globalization can incline nations to bend to diplomacy. In diplomacy, perhaps we can find a moral sense about each other that would provide a forum for compassion.

A forum for compassion is vital. Just as we individually live in both our First and Second Natures, so too, "Our intergroup relations are . . . inherently ambivalent: a hostile undertone is often combined with a desire for harmony."[10] As we have been saying throughout this book, we are bodily built with the means to handle hostility. Now is the time to practice what we know we can do: own our Second Natures and transform them. Only then can we, living in a redeemed First Nature, maintain cooperation among our nations.

Political forces, too, are encouraging us to live and love globally. President Barack Obama, in his book *The Audacity of Hope*, calls for a brand of politics that is rooted in the faith, inclusiveness, and nobility of spirit at the heart of our nation. What he offers is his assessment "of the ways we can ground our politics in the notion of a common good."[11] Underlying his assessment is a search for connection between people. To the extent that human interconnectedness is the foundation for a radically hopeful political consensus, Obama's view challenges all of us to turn toward a world of compassion.

In the words of biologist and ethologist Frans de Waal:

> If we could manage to see people on other continents as part of us, drawing them into our circle of reciprocity and empathy, we would be building upon, rather than going against, our nature [our First Nature]. . . . Empathy is the one weapon in the human repertoire able to rid us of the curse of xenophobia. Empathy is fragile, though. In our close relatives it is switched on by events within their community, such as a youngster in distress, but it is just as easily switched off with regard to outsiders or members of other species, such as prey.[12]

This brings us to the second general answer to our question: When can we learn to live and love globally?

We learn when we see role models. We now know that we are biologically designed to do so. When we see people living from sacred Desire, our mirror neurons facilitate our vicarious experience of their lives.

One such person is Abraham George, born in Kerala and educated in the United States, where he made a fortune. In 1998 he returned to India to establish, among other things, a school for untouchable children. When Thomas Friedman visited George's school and saw the energized children, he thought, "We must have more Abraham Georges—everywhere—by the thousands: people who gaze upon a classroom of untouchable kids and not only see the greatness in each of them but, more important, get them to see the greatness in themselves while endowing them with the tools to bring that out."[13]

This brings us to a question underlying the answer of *seeing* role models—the question of *being* role models. How can each of us *be* a role model of living and loving globally? We offer this answer: Since we are all interrelated, our moral identity is dependent "on the mutual experience of emotions where we co-create each other in ongoing self/other-organization as we live together."[14] Science supports this answer with its understanding of our human social engagement system that is inherently connected to our autonomic physiology. It also supports this answer with the discovery of mirror neurons, the means by which we co-create each other. Our mirror neurons allow us to simulate a role model in our own body. In essence, we live that role model. When our role model is a loving person, our body releases oxytocin that we experience as love.

WHOLENESS AND UNITY

Co-creating each other as loving beings, we draw others around the world into our circle of interconnectedness. We see the world as one circle, as whole, as holy. Not surprisingly, the root of our word *holy* is related to the Old English term for "whole," and "whole" comes from the Middle English *hool,* meaning healthy, unhurt, entire. As we move into the holy that is both beyond and more deeply within us than we can grasp, we begin to understand—or at least we are confronted with the mystery—that humanity, the holy, and creation are interconnected. In short, we are whole. But somehow in the course of human history, including our own personal history, we have forgotten that.

In his book *The Break-Out Principle*, Herbert Benson, MD, talks about the "placebo effect." Instead of writing off the healing that people experience when taking sugar or "dummy" pills as a fluke of the imagination, Benson maintains that healing or significant improvement of health is due to the "healing power of belief" (by the patient, by the physician or healer, and in the relationship between them). As such, he proposes that the placebo effect be renamed "remembered wellness."[15]

Likewise, our growing awareness of the interconnectedness (or, more accurately, the "unity") of all that exists might be thought of as "remembered *wholeness*." That awareness causes us to remember, as Gerald May so eloquently puts it, "the unfathomable, mysteriously intimate co-participation of 'God [the Divine] in me, I in God [the Divine].'"[16] We are not trying to create or envision something that never was; we are seeking to remember—by literally re-membering our brains into neural integration—the reality of creation and the holy as interrelated. Remembering interrelatedness supports our capacity to view the world (and humanity) as a unity; forgetting interrelatedness fosters a view of the world as split between either good or evil.

Perhaps we should pause to consider what we mean by unity. Most of the time, because we are going back and forth between our First and Second Nature, we do not see unity. In our most advanced redeemed First Nature, we might fleetingly glimpse unity and see that it is a reality. It is neither good nor evil. In our search to understand unity, we came across an ancient story recounted by Benedictine Sister Joan Chittister:

> Once upon a time, the story begins, some seekers from the city asked the local monastic a question:
> "How does one seek union with God [the Divine]?"
> And the Wise One said, "The harder you seek, the more distance you create between God [the Divine] and you."
> "So what does one do about the distance?" the seekers asked.

THE NATURE OF BEING HUMAN

Naturally, we live in both our First and our Second Natures. When we live in our Second Nature, we can be restored to our First Nature by reparation within resonant attuning. Reparation is a process of healing wounds that have been caused by someone dissonantly attuning to us.

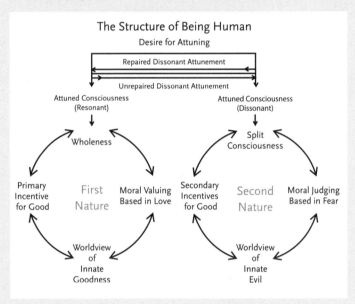

When the wounds occur in the necessary process of socialization, they are relatively easy to repair. Reparation of traumatic dissonant attuning experiences is more difficult. It requires a profound, emotional re-experiencing of the dissonant attuning over time with a person whom we can trust and who is resonantly attuning to us.

Not only can we move from our Second Nature to our First Nature, but we can also be pulled from our First Nature into our Second Nature by unrepaired dissonant attuning. We experience

And the elder said simply, "Just understand that it isn't there."

"Does that mean that God [the Divine] and I are one?" the disciples said.

And the monastic said, "Not one. Not two."

"But how is that possible?" the seekers insisted.

And the monastic answered, "Just like the sun and its light, the ocean and the wave, the singer and the song. Not one. But not two."[17]

"Not one. But not two," describes the nature of our sacred Desire and its relationship to the sacred Desire of others and to the Divine.[18] "Not one. But not two," says that our sacred Desire is not the same as anyone else because no two beings are exactly alike. Nor is it different because the sacred Desire of each of us is

the other as a threat, and our bodies automatically prepare us to fight/flee or freeze.

When people who are living in their First Nature interact with people who are living in their Second Nature, partial effects can result. For example, a person living in Second Nature may glimpse First Nature but not be transformed, or a person living in First Nature can be distorted but not totally drawn into Second Nature.

The point is that we live in both natures. Our challenge is to see both the resonance and the dissonance in our person and in our world without bitterness but with compassion. Compassion enables us to take responsibility for what has caused us to develop our Second Nature, to repair our wounds caused by dissonant attuning experiences, and to live in a redeemed First Nature, where morally we love and value our human nature, and we give others permission to do the same. Living in a redeemed First Nature, we take our incarnated Spirit into our communities, and we live into a worldview of unity.

Source: Nancy K. Morrison and Sally K. Severino, "The Biology of Morality," *Zygon: Journal of Religion and Science* 38, no. 4 (2003): 855–69.

the same as that of all human beings. And we are all in relationship with all others; we are each part of one divinity.

If this is difficult to grasp, it is because we cannot describe the unity of our Desire with the Divine. Instead, we experience it. In order to put an experience into words, we must separate from it. But, unity of our sacred Desire with the Divine is a state-of-being-not-separate: "Not one. But not two." It is objectivity and subjectivity together in being. True unity is resonantly and redemptively attuning to our sacred Desire that is one with the Divine. Human and transhuman are a unity. We can't adequately put it into words. But we can experience it.

How do we know that we are resonantly and redemptively attuning to our sacred Desire? We know it by experiencing the "when" and the "what" of the Divine.

The "when" of the Divine. This happens the moment that we live the direct experience of our self as being in harmony with the Divine. When the good of all becomes the motive of our being, we feel our unity with the Divine in the *subjective* present moment.

The "what" of the Divine. This has an *objective aspect* in addition to a *subjective aspect.* The *objective aspect* is partially mysterious. By its very nature, it cannot totally be elucidated. It is like the unity of matter with energy. We can see the matter, but we can see only the results of energy. Similarly we cannot totally know the mystery of the Divine. But, we can see the results (the objective "what") of the Divine, and they include such things as compassion, mutual accountability, forgiveness, care for the powerless, and the wonder of every moment of life. These reveal a picture of the Divine that is not just anything. It is specific. It is the Divine that exists in all persons and the Divine that is greater than the sum of the Divine in all persons. It is the Divine that has been described by spiritual traditions like the story told by Joan Chittister.

The *subjective aspect* is our experience of joy and gratitude. This is what we experience when our sacred Desire is aligned with the Divine. Human beings need joy, and our brains are designed for joy. Joy is a product of resonant and redemptive attuning that floods our being in all aspects (our biological, our psychological, our sociological, and our spiritual aspects). Joy is generated in an exchange of mutually experienced resonant and redemptive attuning with another. This attuning with each other moves us further toward unity with the Divine, where our intent and our action are in harmony. In unity we experience reality, whether it is pleasure or pain, rather than trying to change reality by either pulling pleasure toward us or pushing pain away. This experience of reality in a state of unity with the Divine is the source of joy. In this state we live most fully who we uniquely are.

John Shelby Spong, spokesperson for one kind of scholarly Christianity, puts it this way,

> We were created neither in . . . original goodness . . . , nor in . . . original sin. . . . Rather, we have evolved into a status . . . a little higher than the ape's. . . . There is a vast contrast between . . . being fallen creatures and . . . being incomplete creatures. Our humanity . . . is . . . distorted by the unfinished nature of our humanity. . . . [W]e do not yet know what it means to be human, since that is a status we have not yet fully achieved.[19]

WHOLENESS AND INTEGRITY-OF-WHOLENESS

At first glance, Spong's "incompleteness" seems to contradict our "remembered wholeness." This brings us to the difference between wholeness and integrity-of-wholeness. *Whole* means all the pieces are there. *Integrity* means complete or our pieces are undivided, a unity. We are born with the potential for integrity-of-wholeness where our sacred Desire and our body are undivided. But when our sacred Desire is not nourished through resonant and redemptive attuning, we become divided within. We are still whole: both our Desire and body exist, but they lack integrity. We have lost integrity-of-wholeness; we have lost unity. Our bodies carry that division into interactions with others, where our biology distorts the expression of our Desire and distorts all we touch, thereby diminishing integrity-of-wholeness in our world. This lack of unity, what Spong calls incompleteness, gives rise to evil.

When we lack unity, our behavior—like the behavior of the mountain climbers who left David Sharp to die—is an offense that not only distorts our Desire but also distorts our expression of the Divine. When we live in unity where the Divine is in us and we are in the Divine, then we bring the Divine, undistorted, to all who—using their mirror neurons—attune to our actions and intentions. When we act with compassion—with integrity-of-wholeness—others will attune to compassion, and we will come to live and love globally. We will live in a shared human identity, and we will live into a new worldview that transcends either a worldview of good (see "First Nature," page 44) or a worldview of evil (Second Nature—see "Second Nature," page 50).

We will live into a worldview of unity (see "The Nature of Being Human," page 148), which frees us to see evil as arising from our having not yet returned to integrity-of-wholeness. We have not yet remembered our original unity. Evil, like good, is real, and it exists in others and ourselves. Viewing the world as a unity calls us to embrace our evil that we bring into the world when we live in our Second Nature. It calls us to embrace the suffering that our evil causes so that we can love it as a signal of something we must claim rather than destroy. Thomas Merton puts it well: "We must try to accept ourselves, whether individually or collectively, not only as perfectly good or perfectly bad, but in our mysterious, unaccountable mixture of good and evil."[20] By claiming and transforming ourselves, we encourage ourselves to live with more integrity-of-wholeness.

When we extend this worldview of unity to others, we view all believers of all faiths as one body moving together toward one ultimate reality, one incarnated spirit, one nondual eternal state of being. We give permission to all people to plumb the depths of their faith traditions, and we share with each other the truths we find. Our sharing becomes a sacred meal where we help each other transform the evil that arises from our evolving nature and where we rejoice in our mutual nourishment.

This is how our sacred Desire brings us back into re-membered integrity-of-wholeness where we live in harmony with the life force of the universe and with each other. Our mirror neurons allow us to share a neural state that is realized in two bodies. Re-membering now takes on a biological meaning as our brain mediates the changes that occur in us. As we transform our worldview of split good or evil into one of unity, our physiology changes from one of fear to one of love. Our autonomic nervous system shifts from either sympathetic (fight/flight) or dorsal vagal (freeze) reactions to ventral vagal regulation of social cuing. This allows our brains, literally, to grow new brain cells and make new neural connections as we re-member our brains into more complex integration and ourselves into evolving integrity-of-wholeness. This is how trusting our sacred Desire truly sets us on a path to a world of compassion.

This challenges us to accept the fact that no matter how much we try—or how much we want to believe that we do—none of us manages to live our lives from the worldview of unity at all times. But hopefully we strive to keep that vision before us, trusting that the holy will guide and strengthen us—and help us forgive ourselves when we fail—to live and love globally.

Though sorting through and fully understanding the implications of our every action as well as every action of governments, businesses, and other entities is undeniably overwhelming and impossible, we must nonetheless seek to discern the movement—and call—of sacred Desire in our lives and in the lives of those near and far. Despite the human penchant for self-delusion and rationalization, we must continually ask ourselves this question: Is the energy of creation flowing through my being and my doing now, in this very moment? This question is both the most challenging and potentially freeing query we will ever ask or be asked. As we understand and live out our own unique expression of the heart of compassion, we enter an awareness that the common good arises from our good and the good of all creation. While the transformation and healing of the world begins within us, it also involves others—mind to mind, brain to brain, and spirit to spirit. For when we live from our sacred Desire, we transform the world from within and between each one of us.

When we truly realize that we are part of an emerging life force and that we share one environment with all other interrelated things, we can naturally cooperate with creation. "This love is not the absolute Good beyond being, but is the depth and height, the length and breadth of being itself."[21] We acknowledge that no God up above will rescue us from our thinning ozone layer, our rising surface temperatures on the earth, our social traumas that affect the physiology, behavior, and culture of animals and humans over generations. Only we, who embody the life force, can let that force flow through us into our world to create it anew with less fear, more equitable use of goods, and more compassionate concern for the downtrodden.

When we care for creation, we move the world slowly toward unity, one person at a time, sharing a common hope in the ultimate goodness of our being. When we love one another, we shape each other in that moment in a way that defines us and our culture as holy. A worldview of unity promotes diplomacy—a common ground for all the forces moving us toward compassion.

In our bodies, diplomacy translates into a physiology where our vasopressin-cortisol system (instills courage) is balanced with our oxytocin system (instills friendliness), our ventral vagal nervous system for social cuing predominates, and our mirror neurons for resonant and redemptive attuning connect us with one another in compassion. In other words, we live in love for the peaceful preservation and nurturance of our world community and our planet.

In our world, diplomacy translates into interdependency. As a result of our interdependency, diplomacy is not just a must; it is also being conditioned. The globalization of our world is encouraging us to talk to each other across cultural differences and to change our concrete and ingrained ideas about each other. The flattening of our world is making immorality (power over others) dangerous and morality (co-creating each other) advantageous. Refining and redefining economic, social, and political dynamics offers us an opportunity for spiritual change.

Spiritual change, which is also psychological and biological change, offers us the opportunity to grow beyond bonds of ethnicity and blood into bonds of trust in each other and in our sacred Desire to connect with what is good. Bonds of trust in each other and in our sacred Desire are not enough to stop terrorist threats, reverse a falling economy, or provide healthcare to all in need. But they are where we start to live and love globally.

Trusting sacred Desire is where a world of compassion begins.

Glossary

Attuning: A special form of social perception and communication whereby we nonverbally know and reflect back the internal subjective state of another; how we biologically, psychologically, and spiritually connect with another.

Resonant attuning: Connecting in harmony with the subjectivity of another.

Dissonant attuning: Connecting in disharmony with the subjectivity of another.

Redemptive attuning: Connecting in harmony with the subjectivity of another but with an increased awareness of how resonant attuning sustains and preserves the goodness in relationship; transforms us to a new being.

Fear of goodness: Fear of our goodness experienced when we are in our Second Nature where

1. our sacred Desire is met with dissonant attuning that remains unrepaired resulting in our split awareness; and

2. our sacred Desire becomes distorted by fear/shame and becomes a part of our self that is despised/enraged.

Fear for goodness: Fear for our goodness experienced when we are in our redeemed First Nature where we are

1. aware that goodness can be harmed, and

2. we are concerned to maintain our goodness and the goodness of all.

First Nature: Living in a state of goodness and wholeness based in love.

Biologically—our parasympathetic ventral vagal system is activated and oxytocin is released.

Psychologically—secure attachment patterns are established, and our minds can tell coherent autobiographical narratives about our psychological and social circumstances.

Spiritually—we love and feel loved.

First Nature worldview: a conviction that

1. goodness and striving for integrity are primary;

2. violence is a reaction to the frustration of our desire for resonant attuning;

3. violence neither fixes things nor restores us; it creates more violence; and

4. violence need not be expressed as such but can be managed within our relationships by being recognized, owned, and repaired.

First Nature morality: Expresses valuing based in love.

Incarnated spirit: A nondual state of being one with the Divine.

Morality: The ability to determine the "rightness" or "wrongness" of our actions based on both following rules and also on knowing the impact of our actions on another through resonant attuning.

Primary incentive for good: The wish to *be* good so that in connection we bring pleasure to another, experience pleasure with another, and sustain the goodness of both.

Redeemed First Nature: First Nature with growing awareness that our subjectivities are connected; we want to preserve the goodness of resonant attuning in order to

1. experience joy and

2. not cause suffering.

Redemptive awareness: Understanding that when we inflict hurt, we both send hurt into the other and also send the experience of being the perpetrator into the other.

Reparation: Healing states of split awareness resulting from dissonant attuning through a process of reliving those states in relationships of resonant attuning.

Sacred Desire: The urge to connect and be one through resonant and redemptive attuning with the Divine in the universe and in each other.

Secondary incentives for good: The ways we try to *do* good in order to avoid losing the potential for resonant attuning; compromised behaviors to stay in relationship when our sacred Desire is distorted by fear/shame.

Second Nature: Living in a state of split awareness and brokenness based in fear.

Biologically—our sympathetic nervous system is activated and vasopressin plus adrenaline and noradrenalin are released.

Psychologically—insecure and disorganized/disoriented attachment patterns are established and our minds cannot tell coherent autobiographical narratives about our psychological and social circumstances.

Spiritually—we want control and we would like to feel powerful.

Second Nature morality: Expresses judging based in fear.

Second Nature worldview: A conviction that

1. evil is primary and inevitable;

2. violence is inherent in our being; we are born with destructive impulses;

3. violence can be managed only by channeling its expression; and

4. violence fixes things.

Trauma: Injury caused in two ways:

1. when dissonant attuning is persistent and remains unrepaired;

2. when dissonant attuning overwhelms our usual coping mechanisms and is perceived as life-threatening, such as what results from physical, sexual, or emotional abuse.

Transformation: The process of changing from a state of fear to a state of love and from Second Nature to First Nature.

Acknowledgments

I N PART, WE DERIVED OUR MODEL of the psychobiospiritual person and our understanding of the essence of human nature from empirical sources—controlled experiments, statistical analyses, and a systematic investigation of scientific claims—when they were available. In our eagerness to make the information accessible, we undoubtedly have oversimplified issues.

We also built our model from work with patients and colleagues, and from our experiences of living as women, mothers, and practitioners of Christian contemplation. All our stories are true. Where needed, in order to protect the confidentiality of those who have shared their experiences with us, we have changed their names and the identifying circumstances. We thank those who allowed us to tell their stories.

We have also drawn illustrative examples from the literature. In instances where we may have misunderstood the authors cited, we apologize. We also apologize for those instances where the influence of others became so much a part of us that we may have overlooked acknowledging the source.

In our clinical work, teaching, and presentations we have learned something about how richly healing resonant attuning can be. We have also learned that the wounds we all carry from dissonant experiences can be touched upon and emerge unexpectedly with pain and hunger. The good news is that these experiences, while painful, can open the path to emotional and spiritual healing.

We are grateful for those who have helped bring this book to fruition. To Jean Blomquist, who walked with us, and to Roy

Carlisle, who encouraged us to keep walking. To Beth Hadas and
Julie Reichert for helping us find our voice. To Cindy Williams,
MD, Ian Osborne, MD, and the Reverend Brian Taylor for reading
our manuscript and pointing out its strengths and weaknesses.
To Paula Huston, who introduced us to two theologians: to Ivan
Illich, who endorsed the original spiritual purpose of our bodies
and minds, and to Hans Urs von Balthasar, whose thesis is that
Christianity can be understood only in light of an immense and
merciful Divine love, a reflection of which is the intensely loving relationship between good caregiver and infant. To the Riven-
dell Community for hosting a workshop where we could share
our ideas and refine our concepts. To Lisa Dale Norton for helping us develop a proposal acceptable to the Templeton Foundation
Press and for her suggestions throughout the book. Most deeply
we appreciate Natalie Lyons Silver, our editor, for her partnership
through the process that improved our book in countless ways.
And to the entire team of Templeton Foundation Press, our sin-
cere thanks for your support in the production of *Sacred Desire:
Growing in Compassionate Living.*

Finally, a book emerges from the lives of the authors. We thank
those who have surrounded us with resonant attuning so that we
could write this book, especially Syble Seckinger and Evelyn Miller
for their abiding encouragement.

Notes

INTRODUCTION

1. Thomas Keating, *Open Mind, Open Heart: The Contemplative Dimension of the Gospel* (New York: Continuum, 1995), 4.

2. Scientific research suggests that Christian contemplative prayer and Buddhist meditation produce similar changes in the brains of practitioners (See "The Science of First Nature," page 44).

3. Daniel J. Siegel, MD, says that mindfulness practices promote awareness of ongoing experience that creates an attunement, or resonance, within the practitioner that harnesses specific social and emotional circuits in the brain. Stimulation of these "resonance circuits" encourages growth that transforms a moment-to-moment state of mindfulness awareness into a long-term state of resilience reflected in enhanced body functions such as healing, immune response, stress reactivity, a general sense of physical well-being, and improved relationships with others. See Daniel J. Siegel, *The Mindful Brain: Reflection and Attunement in the Cultivation of Well-Being* (New York: W. W. Norton, 2007).

4. David Cayley, *Ivan Illich in Conversation* (Concord, Ont.: House of Anansi Press, 1991), 264–65.

1. WOMB OF COMPASSION

1. Martha Ann Kirk, CCVI, *Celebrations of Biblical Women's Stories: Tears, Milk, and Honey* (Kansas City, Mo.: Sheed and Ward, 1987), 7. In her book *Women of Bible Lands*, Kirk writes, "[T]he root word for womb . . . in both Hebrew and Arabic sounds like 'r-h-m'; the root word for womb is also the root word for mercy. A favored Arabic name today is Rahim, which means benevolent or merciful." See Martha Ann Kirk, CCVI, *Women of Bible Lands: A Pilgrimage to Compassion and Wisdom* (Collegeville, Minn.: Liturgical Press, 2004), 144.

2. The power potion is a cocktail that prepares us for fight or flight (see "The Power Potion," page 7).

3. Avivah Gottlieb Zornberg, *The Particulars of Rapture: Reflections on Exodus* (New York: Image/Doubleday, 2000), 337.

4. This experience of compassion is the template for a second womb of compassion that will be co-created after birth, first by mother and infant and then by us and others, and us with the Divine.

5. Daniel N. Stern and Nadia Bruschweiler-Stern, with Alison Freeland, *The Birth of a Mother* (New York: Basic Books, 1998), 37. The Sterns further explain that during the last months of pregnancy a mother-to-be undoes her highly elaborated imagined baby so that when it meets the real baby for the first time there is not a great difference between the two.

6. Oxytocin, a substance first discovered in the pituitary gland by Sir Henry Dale in 1906, speeds up the birthing process and is called "the hormone of calm, love, and healing" by Kerstin Uvnas Moberg, MD, PhD, who is recognized as a world authority on oxytocin (see "The Holy Nectar," page 5).

7. Bruce H. Lipton, *The Biology of Belief: Unleashing the Power of Consciousness, Matter and Miracles* (Santa Rosa, Calif.: Mountain of Love/Elite Books, 2005), 27.

8. Phyllis Tickle, *The Shaping of a Life: A Spiritual Landscape* (New York: Image/Doubleday, 2001), 271–72.

9. Ibid., 272.

10. Francis S. Collins, MD, *The Language of God* (New York: Free Press, 2006), 29.

11. Peter Hobson, professor of developmental psychopathology at the Tavistock Clinic, London, carries our concept of the womb of compassion a step further. He believes that what we call the womb of compassion—the motion and dynamism of the baby's bodily exchanges with other people over the first eighteen months of life—is what gives human beings the capacity to think. The child adds language and self-awareness to the womb of compassion experiences. The process by which human beings learn to think, he says, is a three-step process. First, the infant responds to another. The infant engages with another person in a one-to-one interaction, imitating the other automatically. Second, the infant relates to the world of the other. Side-by-side another, the infant connects with things and events in the world, joining with another person's relatedness to the world. Third, the world

simultaneously has a meaning-for-me and a meaning-for-the-other. The child can be moved to a new orientation toward the world *and* also retain her own initial understanding of things. See Peter Hobson, *The Cradle of Thought: Exploring the Origins of Thinking* (New York: Oxford University Press, 2004).

2. THE GRACE OF GAZING

1. We use the term *gazing* here both in its specific meaning—mother and child intently looking at each other—but also in a more inclusive way that embraces touching, rocking, singing, and talking to the child: those spiritual moments when the Divine becomes visible and palpable through human action and relationship. Also, we're well aware that you personally may feel that you never experienced the grace of gazing, or, given the horrific reality of child abuse today, you may question how we can assume this loving gaze between parent and child is the norm. We will address these issues later, so please keep reading. We believe that this grace-filled gazing is intended for us, which is why we begin here rather than immediately addressing how we humans deviate from the ways of the Divine.

2. When the gazing occurs during nursing, the infant receives not only nourishment but also warming. Nursing stimulates oxytocin, which dilates the blood vessels in the skin of Mother's torso, which in turn warms her infant. See Kerstin Uvnas Moberg, *The Oxytocin Factor: Tapping the Hormone of Calm, Love, and Healing* (Cambridge, Mass.: Da Capo Press, 2003), 94 and 96–97.

3. Despite more fathers assuming this role, mothers remain children's primary caregivers in our culture. We've made a conscious choice to use the term "mother" in this discussion, though we acknowledge, affirm, and celebrate the participation of many caregivers—fathers, grandparents, nannies, and others. An infant's experience of the presence of God begins in the womb, within the mother herself, and continues outside the womb most immediately in relationship with the mother. Because of this, the mother-infant relationship is sacred in a very particular way, and we believe using a generic term should not dilute it. Most of the research findings that we share with you here, or that underlie our observations, are based on mothers and their interactions with their children. Much research remains to be done on the role and

relationship of fathers to children, especially infants. Suffice it to say, we believe that fathers also have a sacred role in the lives of their children and should be fully involved in caring for and nurturing them.

4. James W. Fowler, *Stages of Faith: The Psychology of Human Development and the Quest for Meaning* (San Francisco: Harper and Row, 1981), 16. Fowler writes: "Our first experiences of faith and faithfulness begin at birth. We are received and welcomed with some degree of fidelity by those who care for us. By their consistency in providing for our needs, by their making a valued place for us in their lives, those who welcome us provide an initial experience of loyalty and dependability. And before we can use language, form concepts or even be said to be conscious, we begin to form our first rudimentary intuitions of what the world is like, of how it regards us and of whether we can be 'at home' here" (16).

5. Hobson, *The Cradle of Thought*, 73, 75.

6. Dag Hammarskjöld, *Markings*, trans. Leif Sjöberg and W. H. Auden (New York: Ballantine, 1983), 180.

7. Harry Stack Sullivan, MD, *The Interpersonal Theory of Psychiatry* (New York: W. W. Norton, 1953), 59.

8. Stephen W. Porges, "Social Engagement and Attachment: A Phylogenetic Perspective," *Annals of the New York Academy of Science* 1008 (2003): 31–47.

9. Perhaps even in utero: "Curiously, an additional group of sensory nerves follow the vagus branch. These are sensory nerves from the uterus and mammary glands, as well as probably from the skin on the chest . . . these nerves do not convey their messages through the spinal cord but reach other low parts of the central nervous system directly. They probably do not convey precise information about the location of touch, but more likely influence the deeper parts of the brain that deal with feelings and physiological reactions." See Moberg, *The Oxytocin Factor*, 44.

10. The English Anchoress at St. Julian, Norwich Church, received a revelation from God on May 8, 1373. In her account of that revelation she uses the term "oneing" in much the same way we do: "In the knitting and the oneing . . . 'I am loving you, and you are loving me: and our loving shall never be parted in two.'" Julian of Norwich, *Revelation of Love*, trans. John Skinner (New York: Image Books/Doubleday, 1996), 128–29.

11. You may be familiar with the work of René Spitz, who in the 1940s chronicled the lives of children in a Mexican foundling home. The children were adequately fed and kept clean and warm. However, they were not hugged or held, and because staff members were constantly shifted around, the children were unable to develop stable, loving relationships with particular caregivers. Children who were robust, cheerful infants and toddlers at admission to the home looked like concentration camp victims months later. Some literally died for lack of touch and relationships with consistent, reliable caregivers. (We might also say they died for lack of resonant attuning.) More recently, in the 1990s, a similar situation in Romanian orphanages made international news.

Studies in different countries show that deprivation of relationships in orphanages affect children even after adoption. However, one study in particular showed that training orphanage caregivers to be warm and responsive to the children and having them work regularly with the same children affected not only the children but also the caregivers. The caregivers showed increased socially responsive caregiving behaviors, and the children showed improvements in physical growth, cognition, language development, motor skills, personal-social skills, and affect. See Christina J. Groark, Rifkat J. Muhamedrahimov, Oleg I. Palmov, Natalia V. Nikiforova, and Robert B. McCall, "Improvements in Early Care in Russian Orphanages and Their Relationship to Observed Behaviors," *Infant Mental Health Journal* 26, no. 2 (2005): 96–109.

3. THE WIDENING BOUNDARIES OF LIFE AND LOVE

1. Stephen W. Porges, "Neuroception: A Subconscious System for Detecting Threats and Safety," *Zero to Three* (May 2004): 19–24.

2. Vittorio Gallese, "The Manifold Nature of Interpersonal Relations: The Quest for a Common Mechanism," *Philosophical Transactions of the Royal Society of London* 358 (2003): 517–28.

3. While the entire brain grows rapidly in the first years of human life, the right hemisphere grows especially fast during the first year—establishing the neurobiological origins of the self and emotional regulation. At about eighteen months of life, accelerated growth of our brain shifts from the right to the left hemisphere—allowing for the development of verbal language and the ability to know that another person is a human being with feelings and intentions.

4. Daniel J. Siegel, *The Developing Mind: Toward a Neurobiology of Interpersonal Experience* (New York: Guilford Press, 1999), 140.

5. Stanley I. Greenspan, *The Growth of the Mind and the Endangered Origins of Intelligence* (Reading, Mass.: Perseus Books, 1997), 2, 3.

6. Ibid.

7. Ibid., 62.

4. LIVING IN SACRED DESIRE

1. Siegel, *The Developing Mind*, 272–73.

2. Sharon Begley, *Train Your Mind, Change Your Brain* (New York: Ballantine Books, 2008), 192.

3. Khaled Abou El Fadl, *The Great Theft: Wrestling Islam from the Extremists* (San Francisco: HarperSanFrancisco, 2005), 123.

4. Luke 10:30–35. All biblical citations are from the *New Revised Standard Version of the Holy Bible* (Grand Rapids, Mich.: Zondervan Publishing, 1993) and will be noted parenthetically in the text.

5. Nancy K. Morrison and Sally K. Severino, "Moral Values: Development and Gender Influences," *Journal of the American Academy of Psychoanalysis* 25, no. 2 (1997): 255–75.

6. Bernard McGinn, ed., *Meister Eckhart: Teacher and Preacher* (Mahwah, N.J.: Paulist Press, 1986), 334.

7. C. S. Lewis, *The Lion, the Witch and the Wardrobe* (1950; New York: Harper Trophy 1994), 68.

8. Leonard A. Wisneski and Lucy Anderson, *The Scientific Basis of Integrative Medicine* (New York: CRC Press, 2005), 171.

9. Nancy K. Morrison and Sally K. Severino, "The Biology of Morality," *Zygon: Journal of Religion and Science* 38, no. 4 (2003): 855–69.

10. Psychiatrist Daniel N. Stern calls the mutual belonging to one another "intersubjectivity." He defines *intersubjectivity* as the desire to be known and to share what it feels like to be who we are. He suggests that this desire is universal and innate, though it requires environmental shaping. Daniel N. Stern, *The Present Moment: In Psychotherapy and Everyday Life* (New York: W. W. Norton, 2004), 97.

11. Sally K. Severino and Nancy K. Morrison, "The Myth of Redemptive Violence: Implications for Developmental Theory and Clinical Practice," *Journal of the American Academy of Psychoanalysis* 27, no. 1 (1999): 7–22.

5. THE DISTORTION OF DESIRE

1. Erik Hesse and Mary Main, "Disorganized Infant, Child, and Adult Attachment: Collapse in Behavioral and Attentional Strategies," *Journal of the American Psychoanalytic Association* 48, no. 4 (2000): 1097–1127.
2. Morrison and Severino, "Moral Values," 255–75.
3. Severino and Morrison, "Myth of Redemptive Violence," 7–22.
4. Walter Wink, *Engaging the Powers* (Minneapolis: Fortress Press, 1992), 270.
5. Morrison and Severino, "Biology of Morality," 855–69.
6. Kathryn Watterson, *Not by the Sword* (Boston: Northeastern University Press, 2001), 9.
7. Morrison and Severino, "Moral Values," 270–71.

6. BEYOND DISTORTION

1. Thich Nhat Hanh, *Going Home: Jesus and Buddha as Brothers* (New York: Riverhead Books, 1999), 161.
2. Morrison and Severino, "Moral Values," 273.

7. THE HEALING POWER OF DESIRE

1. David V. Erdman, ed., *The Complete Poetry and Prose of William Blake* (New York: Anchor Books, 1988), 12–13.
2. Rita Nakashima Brock, *Journeys by Heart: A Christology of Erotic Power* (New York: Crossroad Publishing, 1996), 16.
3. "To put it another way, the site from which love can be observed and generated cannot itself lie outside of love . . . ; it can lie only there, where the matter itself lies—namely, in the drama of love." Hans Urs von Balthasar, *Love Alone Is Credible*, trans. D. C. Schindler (1963; San Francisco: Ignatius Press, 2004), 82.
4. "Divine Love can appear in such an overwhelming way that its glorious majesty throws one to the ground; it shines out as the last word and leaves one no choice but to respond in the mode of pure, blind obedience. Nevertheless, both the word and the response acquire their meaning only through a gift from the eternal Person to the finite person, a gift that includes the ability to respond as a finite creature to the infinite, and whose heart and essence is love." Ibid., 56–57.

5. *Be Friends of God: Spiritual Reading from Gregory the Great,* trans. John Leinenweber (Cambridge, Mass.: Cowley Publications, 1990), 145.
6. David W. Augsburger, *Helping People Forgive* (Louisville, Ky.: Westminster John Knox Press, 1996).
7, Gerald May, *Will and Spirit* (1982; New York: HarperCollins, 1987).
8. Stern, *The Present Moment,* 245.
9. Marianne Williamson, *A Return to Love* (New York: HarperCollins, 1996), 190–91.

8. REDEMPTIVE ATTUNING

1. Elizabeth Goudge, *The Child from the Sea* (New York: Coward-McCann, 1970), 462. The "moment of meeting" took place during the seventeenth century on a cold London street one night when Lord Taafe (walking alone in despair of poverty and evil) encountered a stranger (also suffering from hunger and fatigue). The stranger gave Lord Taafe a ring with which to buy a bottle of wine and a loaf of bread upon which they feasted in Lord Taafe's attic room. As they talked and ate, Lord Taafe experienced a love and extraordinary unity with his guest—a redemptive attuning experience—which taught him that God [the Divine] and the old man were indivisible. In other words, while eating the bread and drinking the wine with the stranger, Lord Taafe experienced God's presence in the encounter. As God became visible in the old man, Lord Taafe entered a new—a redeemed—dimension of life in which his despair ended.
2. Mark A. McIntosh, *Discernment and Truth: The Spirituality and Theology of Knowledge* (New York: Crossroad, 2004), 9.
3. Joseph F. Schmidt, FSC, *Everything Is Grace: The Life and Way of Thérèse of Lisieux* (Ijamsville, Md.: The Word Among Us Press, 2007), 42–43.
4. David H. Kelsey, *Imagining Redemption* (Louisville, Ky.: Westminster John Knox Press, 2005), 96.
5. Jack Kornfield, *After the Ecstasy, the Laundry* (New York: Bantam Books, 2000), 235–36.
6. Daniel Goleman, narrator, *Destructive Emotions: How Can We Overcome Them? A Scientific Dialogue with the Dalai Lama* (New York: Bantam Books, 2003).
7. Ivan Illich and David Cayley, *The Rivers North of the Future: The Testament of Ivan Illich as told to David Cayley* (Toronto: House of Anansi Press, 2005), 97.

8. Gary W. Kraemer, Michael H. Ebert, Dennis E. Schmidt, and William T. McKinney, "Strangers in a Strange Land: A Psychobiological Study of Infant Monkeys Before and After Separation from Real or Inanimate Mothers," *Child Development* 62 (1991): 561. See also W. T. Greenough, J. E. Black, and C. S. Wallace, "Experience and Brain Development," *Child Development* 58 (1987): 539–59.

9. Miriam Pollard, OCSO, *The Other Face of Love: Dialogues with the Prison Experience of Albert Speer* (New York: Crossroad Publishing, 1966), 12. Subsequent page numbers appear in the text.

10. von Balthasar, *Love Alone Is Credible*, 108.

11. Pollard, *The Other Face of Love*, 146. Subsequent page numbers appear in the text.

12. von Balthasar, *Love Alone Is Credible*, 116–17.

13. Miroslav Volf, *The End of Memory: Remembering Rightly in a Violent World* (Grand Rapids, Mich.: Eerdmans, 2006).

14. Ralph Waldo Emerson, "The Divinity School Address" (1838), in *Selections from Ralph Waldo Emerson*, ed. Stephen E. Whicher (1960; Boston: Houghton Mifflin, 1960), 102.

9. INCARNATED SPIRITS

1. Martin Luther King Jr., "Letter from Birmingham Jail" (1963), in *Why We Can't Wait* (New York: Signet Classic, 2000), 65.

2. His Holiness the Dalai Lama, *The Universe in a Single Atom: The Convergence of Science and Spirituality* (New York: Morgan Road Books, 2005), 199.

3. Edmund Colledge, OSA, and Bernard McGinn, trans., *Meister Eckhart: The Essential Sermons, Commentaries, Treatises, and Defense* (Mahwah, N.J.: Paulist Press, 1981), 132.

4. Bede Griffiths, quoted in Bruno Barnhart, ed., *The One Light: Bede Griffiths' Principal Writings* (Springfield, Ill.: Templegate Publishers, 2001), 140.

5. Stephen W. Porges, "Social Engagement and Attachment: A Phylogenetic Perspective," *Annals of the New York Academy of Science* 1008 (2003): 31–47.

6. Vittorio Gallese, M. N. Eagle, and P. Migone, "Intentional Attunement: Mirror Neurons and the Neural Underpinnings of Interpersonal Relations," *Journal of the American Psychoanalytic Association* 55 (2007): 131–76.

7. James P. Henry and Sheila Wang, "Effects of Early Stress on Adult Affiliative Behavior," *Psychoneuroendocrinology* 23 (1998): 863–75.

8. Ibid.

9. Sheila Wang, "Traumatic Stress and Attachment," *Acta Physiologica Scandinavica* 161 (1997): 164–69; C. Sue Carter, "Neuroendocrine Perspectives on Social Attachment and Love," *Psychoneuroendocrinology* 23 (1998): 779–818.

10. Wang, "Traumatic Stress and Attachment," 166.

11. The Most Rev. Rowan Williams, "God Speaks Our Language," *The Living Church* (December 19, 2004): 12.

12. A current hypothesis holds that people with autism suffer a deficit or malfunctioning of attuning, in turn produced by a dysfunction of their mirror neuron system. See Vittorio Gallese, "Intentional Attunement: A Neurophysiological Perspective on Social Cognition and Its Disruption in Autism," *Brain Research* 1079 (2006): 15–24. It makes sense, then, that engaging with and correcting a malfunctioning system could lead to healing.

13. von Balthasar, *Love Alone Is Credible*, 119.

14. Nancy K. Morrison and Sally K. Severino, "Altruism: Toward a Psychobiospiritual Conceptualization," *Zygon: Journal of Religion and Science* 42, no. 1 (2007): 26.

15. Rabbi Craig H. Ezring, "Rabbi Backs Into Helpful Approach," *Albuquerque Journal*, February 4, 2005, C3.

16. Thomas Keating's presentation at a conference entitled, "Eternal Now and How to Be There," held at the Downtown Hyatt Hotel, Albuquerque, N.M., July 15–18, 2004.

17. Sarah also demonstrated the powerful effects of parental touching, which elicited oxytocin that shifted her from stress (vasopressin, cortisol physiology) to calm physiology. Living in an oxytocin physiology promotes secure attachments and successful learning. Moberg, *The Oxytocin Factor*, 8.

10. TOWARD A WORLD OF COMPASSION

1. von Balthasar, *Love Alone Is Credible*, 128–29.

2. Fyodor Dostoyevsky, *The Brothers Karamazov* (New York: Modern Library, 1992), 334.

3. Kelsey, *Imagining Redemption*, 104.

4. Mark A. McIntosh, *Discernment and Truth: The Spirituality and Theology of Knowledge* (New York: Crossroad Publishing, 2004), 12.

5. Jon Kabat-Zinn, *Coming to Our Senses: Healing Ourselves and the World through Mindfulness* (New York: Hyperion, 2005), 16.

6. von Balthasar, *Love Alone Is Credible*, 133–34.

7. Louis Cozolino, *The Neuroscience of Human Relationships: Attachment and the Developing Social Brain* (New York: W. W. Norton, 2006).

8. Christopher Boehm, *Hierarchy in the Forest: The Evolution of Egalitarian Behavior* (Cambridge, Mass.: Harvard University Press, 2001), 12, 197, 254.

9. Thomas L. Friedman, *The World Is Flat: A Brief History of the Twenty-First Century* (New York: Farrar, Straus and Giroux, 2006).

10. Frans de Waal, *Our Inner Ape* (New York: Riverhead Books, 2005), 148.

11. Barack Obama, *The Audacity of Hope: Thoughts on Reclaiming the American Dream* (New York: Crown, 2006), 9.

12. de Waal, *Our Inner Ape*, 247.

13. Friedman, *The World Is Flat*, 569.

14. Morrison and Severino, "Altruism," 30.

15. Herbert Benson, MD, and William Proctor, *The Break-Out Principle* (New York: Scribner, 2003), 54.

16. Gerald May, MD, *The Dark Night of the Soul: A Psychiatrist Explores the Connection Between Darkness and Spiritual Growth* (San Francisco: HarperSanFrancisco, 2004), 76.

17. Joan Chittister, OBS, *Wisdom Distilled from the Daily* (New York: HarperCollins, 1990), 195.

18. Meister Eckhart used two images to describe Divine action and our collaboration with that action: a mirror and a tub. "Just as the sun is in the mirror but is not the mirror and the mirror manifests the sun but is not the sun, God [the Divine] is both immanent and transcendent." God [the Divine] is in our soul, and our inner reality is the capability of reflecting the divine nature—our God-rays [Divine-rays]. But God [the Divine] transcends our soul. Eckhart used the image of a tub differently, saying that if one fills a tub with water, the water is united with the tub but not one with it. This is not so with the soul, which is one with God [the Divine]. Michael Demkovich, *Introducing Meister Eckhart* (Ottawa: Novalis, 2005), 127–33.

19. John Shelby Spong, *The Sins of Scripture: Exposing the Bible's Texts of Hate to Reveal the God of Love* (New York: HarperCollins, 2005), 177.

20. Thomas Merton, *New Seeds of Contemplation* (New York: New Directions, 1972), 117.

21. von Balthasar, *Love Alone Is Credible*, 145.

Index